Collected Po

Thom Gunn was born in Gravesend in 1929. After National Service, he read English at Trinity College, Cambridge, and had his first book of poems, *Fighting Terms*, published while he was still an undergraduate. He moved to North California in 1954 and now teaches half of each year at Berkeley. He lives in San Francisco.

In 1992, following the publication of *The Man with Night Sweats*, he was awarded the first Forward Prize for Poetry.

by the same author

FIGHTING TERMS
THE SENSE OF MOVEMENT
MY SAD CAPTAINS
POSITIVES
TOUCH
MOLY
JACK STRAW'S CASTLE
SELECTED POEMS 1950–1975
THE PASSAGES OF JOY
THE MAN WITH NIGHT SWEATS

essays

THE OCCASIONS OF POETRY:
ESSAYS IN CRITICISM AND AUTOBIOGRAPHY
SHELF LIFE

Thom Gunn

COLLECTED POEMS

faber and faber

First published in 1993
by Faber and Faber Limited
3 Queen Square London WC1N 3AU
This paperback edition first published in 1994

Printed and bound by Antony Rowe Ltd, Eastbourne, England

A CIP record for this book is available from
the British Library

ISBN 0-571-17195-8

to Mike Kitay

Contents

The Sense of Movement (1957)

My Sad Captains (1961)

Misanthropos (1965)

Poems from the 1960s

Moly (1971)

Jack Straw's Castle (1976)

I

The Passages of Joy (1982)

[xiii]

Poems from the 1980s

The Man with Night Sweats (1992)

I

Fighting Terms (1954)

The Wound

The huge wound in my head began to heal
About the beginning of the seventh week.
Its valleys darkened, its villages became still:
For joy I did not move and dared not speak,
Not doctors would cure it, but time, its patient skill.

And constantly my mind returned to Troy.
After I sailed the seas I fought in turn
On both sides, sharing even Helen's joy
Of place, and growing up – to see Troy burn –
As Neoptolemus, that stubborn boy.

I lay and rested as prescription said.
Manoeuvered with the Greeks, or sallied out
Each day with Hector. Finally my bed
Became Achilles' tent, to which the lout
Thersites came reporting numbers dead.

I was myself: subject to no man's breath:
My own commander was my enemy.
And while my belt hung up, sword in the sheath,
Thersites shambled in and breathlessly
Cackled about my friend Patroclus' death.

I called for armour, rose, and did not reel.
But, when I thought, rage at his noble pain
Flew to my head, and turning I could feel
My wound break open wide. Over again
I had to let those storm-lit valleys heal.

Here Come the Saints

Here come the saints: so near, so innocent
They gravely cross the field of moonlit snow;
We villagers gape humbly at the show.
No act or gesture can suggest intent.
They only wait until the first cock crow
Batters our ears, and with abrupt and violent
Motions into the terrible dark wood they go.

To his Cynical Mistress

And love is then no more than a compromise?
An impermanent treaty waiting to be signed
    By the two enemies?
– While the calculating Cupid feigning impartial blind
Drafts it, promising peace, both leaders wise
To his antics sign but secretly double their spies.

On each side is the ignorant animal nation
Jostling friendly in streets, enjoying in good faith
    This celebration,
Forgetting their enmity with cheers and drunken breath,
But for them there has not been yet amalgamation:
The leaders calmly plot assassination.

Wind in the Street

The same faces, and then the same scandals
Confront me inside the talking shop which I
Frequent for my own good. So the assistant
Points to the old cogwheels, the old handles
Set in machines which to buy would be to buy
The same faces, and then the same scandals.

I climb by the same stairs to a square attic.
And I gasp, for surely this is something new!
So square, so simple. It is new to be so simple.
Then I see the same sky through the skylight, static
Cloudless, the same artificial toylike blue.
The same stairs led to the same attic.

I only came, I explain, to look round,
To the assistant who coos while I regain the street.
Searching thoroughly, I did not see what I wanted.
What I wanted would have been what I found.
My voice carries, his voice blows to his feet:
I only came, I explain, to look round.

I may return, meanwhile I'll look elsewhere:
My want may modify to what I have seen.
So I smile wearily, though even as I smile
A purposeful gust of wind tugs at my hair;
But I turn, I wave, I am not sure what I mean.
I may return, meanwhile I'll look elsewhere.

Lazarus Not Raised

He was not changed. His friends around the grave
Stared down upon his greasy placid face
Bobbing on shadows; nothing it seemed could save
His body now from the sand below their wave,
The scheduled miracle not taking place.

He lay inert beneath those outstretched hands
Which beckoned him to life. Though coffin case
Was ready to hold life and winding bands
At his first stir would loose the frozen glands,
The scheduled miracle did not take place.

O Lazarus, distended body laid
Glittering without weight on death's surface.
Rise now before you sink, we dare not wade
Into that sad marsh where (the mourners cried)
The scheduled miracle cannot take place.

When first aroused and given thoughts and breath
He chose to amble at an easy pace
In childhood fields imaginary and safe –
Much like the trivial territory of death
(The miracle had not yet taken place).

He chose to spend his thoughts like this at first
And disregard the nag of offered grace,
Then chose to spend the rest of them in rest.
The final effort came, forward we pressed
To see the scheduled miracle take place:

Abruptly the corpse blinked and shook his head
Then sank again, sliding without a trace
From sight, to take slime on the deepest bed
Of vacancy. He had chosen to stay dead,
The scheduled miracle did not take place.

Nothing else changed. I saw somebody peer,
Stooping, into the oblong box of space.
His friends had done their best: without such fear,
Without that terrified awakening glare,
The scheduled miracle would have taken place.

Lofty in the Palais de Danse

You are not random picked. I tell you you
Are much like one I knew before, that died.
Shall we sit down, and drink and munch a while
– I want to see if you will really do:
If not we'll get it over now outside.
Wary I wait for one unusual smile.

I never felt this restiveness with her:
I lay calm wanting nothing but what I had.
And now I stand each night outside the Mills
For girls, then shift them to the cinema
Or dance hall . . . Like the world, I've gone to bad.
A deadly world: for, once I like, it kills.

The same with everything: the only posting
I ever liked, was short. And so in me
I kill the easy things that others like
To teach them that no liking can be lasting:
All that you praise I take, what modesty
What gentleness, you ruin while you speak.

And partly that I couldn't if I would
Be bed-content with likenesses so dumb.
Passed in the street, they seem identical
To her original, yet understood
Exhaustively as soon as slept with, some
Lack this, some that, and none like her at all.

You praise my strength. The muscle on my arm.
Yes. Now the other. Yes, about the same.
I've got another muscle you can feel.
Dare say you knew. Only expected harm
Falls from a khaki man. That's why you came
With me and when I go you follow still.

Now that we sway here in the shadowed street
Why can't I keep my mind clenched on the job?
Your body is a good one, not without
Earlier performance, but in this repeat
The pictures are unwilled that I see bob
Out of the dark, and you can't turn them out.

Round and Round

The lighthouse keeper's world is round,
Belongings skipping in a ring –
All that a man may want, therein,
A wife, a wireless, bread, jam, soap,
Yet day by night his straining hope
Shoots out to live upon the sound
The spinning waves make while they break
For their own endeavour's sake –
The lighthouse keeper's world is round.

He wonders, winding up the stair
To work the lamp which lights the ships,
Why each secured possession skips
With face towards the centre turned,
From table-loads of books has learned
Shore-worlds are round as well, not square,
But there things dance with faces out-
ward turned: faces of fear and doubt?
He wonders, winding up the stair.

When it is calm, the rocks are safe
To take a little exercise
But all he does is fix his eyes
On that huge totem he has left
Where thoughts dance round what will not shift –
His secret inarticulate grief.
Waves have no sun, but are beam-caught
Running below his feet, wry salt,
When, in a calm, the rocks are safe.

Helen's Rape

Hers was the last authentic rape:
From forced content of common breeder
Bringing the violent dreamed escape
Which came to her in different shape
Than to Europa, Danaë, Leda:

Paris. He was a man. And yet
That Aphrodite brought this want
Found too implausible to admit:
And so against this story set
The story of a stolen aunt.

Trust man to prevaricate and disguise
A real event when it takes place:
And Romans stifling Sabine cries
To multiply and vulgarize
What even Trojan did with grace.

Helen herself could not through flesh
Abandon flesh; she felt surround
Her absent body, never fresh
The mortal context, and the mesh
Of the continual battle's sound.

The Secret Sharer

Over the ankles in snow and numb past pain
I stared up at my window three stories high:
From a white street unconcerned as a dead eye,
I patiently called my name again and again.

The curtains were lit, through glass were lit by doubt.
And there was I, within the room alone.
In the empty wind I stood and shouted on:
But O, what if the strange head should peer out?

Suspended taut between two equal fears
I was like to be torn apart by their strong pull:
What, I asked, if I never hear my call?
And what if it reaches my insensitive ears?

Fixed in my socket of thought I saw them move
Aside, I saw that some uncertain hand
Had touched the curtains. Mine? I wondered. And,
At this instant, the wind turned in its groove.

The wind turns in its groove and I am here
Lying in bed, the snow and street outside;
Fire-glow still reassuring; dark defied.
The wind turns in its groove: I am still there.

La Prisonnière

Now I will shut you in a box
With massive sides and a lid that locks.
Only by that I can be sure
That you are still mine and mine secure,
And know where you are when I'm not by,
No longer needing to wonder and spy.
I may forget you at party or play
But do not fear I shall keep away
With any Miss Brown or any Miss Jones.
If my return finds a heap of bones –
Too dry to simper, too dry to whine –
You will still be mine and only mine.

Carnal Knowledge

Even in bed I pose: desire may grow
More circumstantial and less circumspect
Each night, but an acute girl would suspect
That my self is not like my body, bare.
I wonder if you know, or, knowing, care?
You know I know you know I know you know.

I am not what I seem, believe me, so
For the magnanimous pagan I pretend
Substitute a forked creature as your friend.
When darkness lies without a roll or stir
Flaccid, you want a competent poseur.
I know you know I know you know I know.

Cackle you hen, and answer when I crow.
No need to grope: I'm still playing the same
Comical act inside the tragic game.
Yet things perhaps are simpler: could it be
A mere tear-jerker void of honesty?
You know I know you know I know you know.

Leave me. Within a minute I will stow
Your greedy mouth, but will not yet to grips.
'There is a space between the breast and lips.'
Also a space between the thighs and head,
So great, we might as well not be in bed.
I know you know I know you know I know.

I hardly hoped for happy thoughts, although
In a most happy sleeping time I dreamt
We did not hold each other in contempt.
Then lifting from my lids night's penny weights
I saw that lack of love contaminates.
You know I know you know I know you know.

Abandon me to stammering, and go;
If you have tears, prepare to cry elsewhere –
I know of no emotion we can share.
Your intellectual protests are a bore
And even now I pose, so now go, for
I know you know.

The Court Revolt

The worst conspired, their differences sunk;
And others joined from weakness or because
Sick boredom had succeeded leisure drunk:
King stork was welcome to replace a log,
They tittered at the thrill, then hushed, agog.

Nor was this doomed king either log, or dead:
Still active, generous, striding through the court.
Suspicion never came into his head.
Not overthrown by system or idea
But individual jealousy and fear.

Yet he was doomed, and not by them alone.
– How can a man hold office in these days?
Not that it is too much for flesh and bone
But flesh and bone are far too much for it:
There needs a something inhuman to fit.

His natural magnanimity would appear
Insulting charity to the subject now.
The subject's real subjection, though, was near:
Coming from justice without face or shape
Was self-subjection which has no escape.

The loyal rescued him one night. What then?
Not write his memoirs in America
Nor take a manual job with foreign men
Nor fight against his country, which he loved.
His links were broken; but were scarcely proved.

Though on a larger scale, see in his case
A problem which is problem of us all:
His human flames of energy had no place –
The grate that they were lit for would not hold,
The vacant grates were destined to be cold.

The Right Possessor

Bandit to prince was his advance one night,
He was soon overthrown, he was exiled.
At daybreak back the roads of his delight
He went deliberately, no longer child.
On either hand leaves withered by his shot,
But all, the weeping trees, all, he forgot.

The devastated country was enlarged,
Villages burnt to nothing, fields of wheat
Flattened, for his soldiers – now discharged –
Had trampled everything beneath their feet.
He did not look, and only checked his stride
Once, on a cartridge belt he kicked aside.

Some orphaned boys were playing in the sun
And helped the tall sad man to find his road.
These boys apart, he hated everyone
Born in this fickle land he had let blood,
And so, indignant, reached the unruined sea,
Jumped in a boat and left the country free.

The years abroad brought bad dreams, he would leap
Shuddering from bed, but seldom mix with men.
Habit of memory between sleep and sleep
Was hardening to fixed ideal, when
A message from the latest government
Recalled this exile from his banishment.

But at the frontier, how the land seemed small!
Calm, neutral, waiting, drifted deep with snow.
He noticed no one noticed him at all,
No widow's looks, no gratitude. Below
His movements set a still indifference:
Forward or backward now made equal sense.

He paced the snow, from cold not expectation,
His footprints obvious in a perfect round.
Then least suspected in that lonely station
A boy ran forward on the frozen ground
And shot the muffled stranger in the head,
Who fell upon the platform and was dead.

The news put all the nation into mourning.
What need to let my conqueror die, she cried?
Why did my contradictory mind keep warning
That loss of dignity lay at his side?
Now indecision and delay have lost
For ever what I always wanted most.

Looking Glass

Remote, it lives now in a tiny glass,
Charmed-still forever at one stage of growing:
Trees are in leaf, and children all day long
Laugh in their effortless continual going
To hidden ends along the ways of grass,
And birds make great perspectives of their song.

I still hold Eden in my garden wall.
It was not innocence lost, not innocence
But a fine callous fickleness which could fix
On every novelty the mind or sense
Reached for, gratification being all,
And closed the tool box for the box of tricks.

I am the gardener now myself, and know,
Though I am free to leave the path and tear
Ripe from the branch the yellows and the reds,
I am responsible for order here
(The time it takes to teach the fruits to grow,
The pains of keeping neat the flower beds).

What little watering I do is pleasure,
I let the birds on pear and apple sup,
I do not use my clippers or my rake,
I do not tie the fallen branches up,
I leave the weeding and employ my leisure
In idling on the lawns or by the lake.

Gardening manuals frown at this neglect
But risks are authorized by such a weather.
What want but water should the flowers need?
I will enjoy the green before it wither,
And do not care if villagers suspect
It goes to seed. How well it goes to seed . . .

I see myself inside a looking glass
Framed there by shadowed trees alive with song
And fruits no sooner noticed than enjoyed;
I take it from my pocket and gaze long,
Forgetting in my pleasure how I pass
From town to town, damp-booted, unemployed.

Lerici

Shelley was drowned near here. Arms at his side
He fell submissive through the waves, and he
Was but a minor conquest of the sea:
The darkness that he met was nurse not bride.

Others make gestures with arms open wide,
Compressing in the minute before death
What great expense of muscle and of breath
They would have made if they had never died.

Byron was worth the sea's pursuit. His touch
Was masterful to water, audience
To which he could react until an end.
Strong swimmers, fishermen, explorers: such
Dignify death by thriftless violence –
Squandering with so little left to spend.

A Mirror for Poets

It was a violent time. Wheels, racks, and fires
In every writer's mouth, and not mere rant.
Certain shrewd herdsmen, between twisted wires
Of penalty folding the realm, were thanked
For organizing spies and secret police
By richness in the flock, which they could fleece.

Hacks in the Fleet and nobles in the Tower:
Shakespeare must keep the peace, and Jonson's thumb
Be branded (for manslaughter), to the power
Of irons the admired Southampton's power was come.
Above all swayed the diseased and doubtful Queen:
Her state canopied by the glamour of pain.

In this society the boundaries met
Of life and life, at danger; with no space
Being left between, except where might be set
That mathematical point whose time and place
Could not exist. Yet at this point they found
Arcadia, a fruitful permanent land.

The faint and stumbling crowds were dim to sight
Who had no time for pity or for terror:
Here moved the Forms, flooding like moonlight,
In which the act or thought perceived its error.
The hustling details, calmed and relevant.
Here mankind might behold its whole extent.

Here in a cave the Paphlagonian King
Crouched, waiting for his greater counterpart
Who one remove from likelihood may seem,
But several nearer to the human heart.
In exile from dimension, change by storm,
Here his huge magnanimity was born.

Yet the historians tell us, life meant less.
It was a violent time, and evil-smelling.
Jonson howled 'Hell's a grammar-school to this,'
But found renunciation well worth telling.
Winnowing with his flail of comedy
He showed coherence in society.

In street, in tavern, happening would cry
'I am myself, but part of something greater,
Find poets what that is, do not pass by,
For feel my fingers in your pia mater.
I am a cruelly insistent friend:
You cannot smile at me and make an end.'

The Beach Head

Now that a letter gives me ground at last
For starting from, I see my enterprise
Is more than application by a blast
Upon a trumpet slung beside a gate,
Security a fraud, and how unwise
Was disembarking on your Welfare State.

What should they see in you but what I see,
These friends you mention whom I do not know?
– You unsuspecting that a refugee
Might want the land complete, write in a tone
Too matter-of-fact, of small affairs below
A minister's seduction of the Crown.

And even if they could be innocent,
They still applaud you, keep you satisfied
And occupy your time, which I resent.
Their werewolf lust and cunning are afraid
Of night-exposure in the hair, so hide
Distant as possible from my palisade.

I have my ground. A brain-sick enemy
Pacing his beach head he so plotted for
Which now seems trivial to his jealousy
And ignorance of the great important part,
I almost wish I had no narrow shore.
I seek a pathway to the country's heart.

Shall I be John a Gaunt and with my band
Of mad bloods pass in one spectacular dash,
Fighting before and after, through your land,
To issue out unharmed the farther side,
With little object other than panache
And showing what great odds may be defied?

That way achievement would at once be history:
Living inside, I would not know the danger:
Hurry is blind and so does not brave mystery;
I should be led to underrate, by haste,
Your natural beauties: while I, hare-brained stranger,
Would not be much distinguished from the rest.

Or shall I wait and calculate my chances
Consolidating this my inch-square base,
– Myself a spy, killing your spies-in-glances –
Planning when you have least supplies or clothing
A pincer-move to end in an embrace,
And risk that your mild liking turn to loathing?

A Kind of Ethics

Old trees are witnesses:
    Their simple religion is forced into the cold,
    No intermediary gives them rules of conduct:
    All day without a minister they hold
Primitive services.

The power that they receive
    Out of the water, air and earth, can be
    Partial at best, for only on their branches
    Where leaves start from the black extremity
Can they be said to live.

The past that they have led
    Makes unapproachable and hidden sin:
    Deep in the foul confusion of their thicket,
    So dense no human being can go in,
Dry tangled twigs lie dead.

Among such broken wood
    Wild animals give birth to sharp-toothed young:
    Unregenerate, they have no time for worship.
    Careless, out of a possibly bad may come
An undeniable good.

Tamer and Hawk

I thought I was so tough,
But gentled at your hands,
Cannot be quick enough
To fly for you and show
That when I go I go
At your commands.

Even in flight above
I am no longer free:
You seeled me with your love,
I am blind to other birds –
The habit of your words
Has hooded me.

As formerly, I wheel
I hover and I twist,
But only want the feel,
In my possessive thought,
Of catcher and of caught
Upon your wrist.

You but half civilize,
Taming me in this way.
Through having only eyes
For you I fear to lose,
I lose to keep, and choose
Tamer as prey.

Captain in Time of Peace

Crudely continues what has been begun
Crudely, because the crude expedient
Sets crude and final what is to be won.
Tactics commit me falsely, what I want
Is not the raising of a siege but this:
　　Honour in the town at peace.

I see you bend your head by the fireplace
Softly examining your outspread hand,
A puzzled look unguarded on your face,
As if you did not fully understand.
How can I with most gentleness explain
　　I will not plot my moves again?

Something I try, and yet when I express
Trite cinema endearments, all is said.
There, I think still in terms of mere success
— Success in raising up your downturned head.
Pity a lumpish soldier out of work,
　　And teach him manners with a look.

And if I cannot gracefully receive
When you are generous, know that the habit
Of soldiers is to loot. So please forgive
All my inadequacy: I was fit
For peaceful living once, and was not born
　　A clumsy brute in uniform.

Without a Counterpart

Last night I woke in fright: you were not there.
I seemed to face across a deep sad plain
Hedged at one end, a hillock in the centre.
And I was chained, to wait and starve alone,
And could not think what I was waiting for.

I lay, peering as best I could, then saw
Two reed-lined ponds, reflections of the sky.
I noticed with a shock a long volcano
Which like a third brimmed-full with darkness lay:
And knew that from its opening death would flow.

Though I could swear I had not been before
Captived or free in this eccentric scene
I knew it well, lonely, peculiar,
Taught it maybe by some forgotten dream.
And somehow guessed that it was right to fear.

My cheek on prickly turf I waited still.
Then the ground shook. I knew the end had come.
The whole plain rose above me like a wall.
And for my prayers I only spoke your name –
All changed at once: I had undone the spell.

The bad hole in the ground no longer gaped –
The hard land round it, flexing into flesh,
Warmed me instead of swallowing me up.
It was your mouth, and all the rest your face.
Your arms still chained me as you fell asleep.

For a Birthday

I have reached a time when words no longer help:
Instead of guiding me across the moors
Strong landmarks in the uncertain out-of-doors,
Or like dependable friars on the Alp
Saving with wisdom and with brandy kegs,
They are gravel-stones, or tiny dogs which yelp
Biting my trousers, running round my legs.

Description and analysis degrade,
Limit, delay, slipped land from what has been;
And when we groan My Darling what we mean
Looked at more closely would too soon evade
The intellectual habit of our eyes;
And either the experience would fade
Or our approximations would be lies.

The snarling dogs are weight upon my haste,
Tons which I am detaching ounce by ounce.
All my agnostic irony I renounce
So I may climb to regions where I rest
In springs of speech, the dark before of truth:
The sweet moist wafer of your tongue I taste,
And find right meanings in your silent mouth.

Incident on a Journey

One night I reached a cave: I slept, my head
Full of the air. There came about daybreak
A red-coat soldier to the mouth, who said
'I am not living, in hell's pains I ache,
    But I regret nothing.'

His forehead had a bloody wound whose streaming
The pallid staring face illuminated.
Whether his words were mine or his, in dreaming
I found they were my deepest thoughts translated.
    '*I regret nothing*:

'Turn your closed eyes to see upon these walls
A mural scratched there by an earlier man,
And coloured with the blood of animals:
Showing humanity beyond its span,
    Regretting nothing.

'No plausible nostalgia, no brown shame
I had when treating with my enemies.
And always when a living impulse came
I acted, and my action made me wise.
    And I regretted nothing.

'I as possessor of unnatural strength
Was hunted, one day netted in a brawl;
A minute far beyond a minute's length
Took from me passion, strength, and life, and all.
    But I regretted nothing.

'Their triumph left my body in the dust;
The dust and beer still clotting in my hair
When I rise lonely, will-less. Where I must
I go, and what I must I bear.
    And I regret nothing.

'My lust runs yet and is unsatisfied,
My hate throbs yet but I am feeble-limbed;
If as an animal I could have died
My death had scattered instinct to the wind,
    Regrets as nothing.'

Later I woke. I started to my feet.
The valley light, the mist already going.
I was alive and felt my body sweet,
Uncaked blood in all its channels flowing.
    I would regret nothing.

The Sense of Movement (1957)

'Je le suis, je veux l'être.'

Auguste in *Cinna*

On the Move

The blue jay scuffling in the bushes follows
Some hidden purpose, and the gust of birds
That spurts across the field, the wheeling swallows,
Has nested in the trees and undergrowth.
Seeking their instinct, or their poise, or both,
One moves with an uncertain violence
Under the dust thrown by a baffled sense
Or the dull thunder of approximate words.

On motorcycles, up the road, they come:
Small, black, as flies hanging in heat, the Boys,
Until the distance throws them forth, their hum
Bulges to thunder held by calf and thigh.
In goggles, donned impersonality,
In gleaming jackets trophied with the dust,
They strap in doubt – by hiding it, robust –
And almost hear a meaning in their noise.

Exact conclusion of their hardiness
Has no shape yet, but from known whereabouts
They ride, direction where the tyres press.
They scare a flight of birds across the field:
Much that is natural, to the will must yield.
Men manufacture both machine and soul,
And use what they imperfectly control
To dare a future from the taken routes.

It is a part solution, after all.
One is not necessarily discord
On earth; or damned because, half animal,
One lacks direct instinct, because one wakes
Afloat on movement that divides and breaks.
One joins the movement in a valueless world,
Choosing it, till, both hurler and the hurled,
One moves as well, always toward, toward.

A minute holds them, who have come to go:
The self-defined, astride the created will
They burst away; the towns they travel through
Are home for neither bird nor holiness,
For birds and saints complete their purposes.
At worst, one is in motion; and at best,
Reaching no absolute, in which to rest,
One is always nearer by not keeping still.

The Nature of an Action

I

Here is a room with heavy-footed chairs,
A glass bell loaded with wax grapes and pears,

A polished table, holding down the look
Of bracket, mantelpiece, and marbled book.

Staying within the cluttered square of fact,
I cannot slip the clumsy fond contact:

So step into the corridor and start,
Directed by the compass of my heart.

2

Although the narrow corridor appears
So short, the journey took me twenty years.

Each gesture that my habit taught me fell
Down to the boards and made an obstacle.

I paused to watch the fly marks on a shelf,
And found the great obstruction of myself.

I reached the end but, pacing back and forth,
I could not see what reaching it was worth.

In corridors the rooms are undefined:
I groped to feel a handle in the mind.

Testing my faculties I found a stealth
Of passive illness lurking in my health.

And though I saw the corridor stretch bare,
Dusty, and hard, I doubted it was there;

Doubted myself, what final evidence
Lay in perceptions or in common sense?

3

My cause lay in the will, that opens straight
Upon an act for the most desperate.

That simple handle found, I entered in
The other room, where I had never been.

I found within it heavy-footed chairs,
A glass bell loaded with wax grapes and pears,

A polished table, holding down the look
Of bracket, mantelpiece, and marbled book.

Much like the first, this room in which I went.
Only my being there is different.

At the Back of the North Wind

All summer's warmth was stored there in the hay;
Below, the troughs of water froze: the boy
Climbed nightly up the rungs behind the stalls
And planted deep between the clothes he heard
The kind wind bluster, but the last he knew
Was sharp and filled his head, the smell of hay.

Here wrapped within the cobbled mews he woke.
Passing from summer, climbing down through winter
He broke into an air that kept no season:
Denying change, for it was always there.
It nipped the memory numb, scalding away
The castle of winter and the smell of hay.

The ostlers knew, but did not tell him more
Than hay is what we turn to. Other smells,
Horses, leather, manure, fresh sweat, and sweet
Mortality, he found them on the North.
That was her sister, East, that shrilled all day
And swept the mews dead clean from wisps of hay.

Before the Carnival

A painting by Carl Timner

Look, in the attic, the unentered room,
A naked boy leans on the outspread knees
Of his tall brother lolling in costume,
Tights, vest, and cap, of one who on trapeze
Finds comfort farthest from complacencies.

Behind the little boy and acrobat
Through circling half-light from their downshed musing
Hurries the miser in his double hat;
The dry guitar he holds is still, abusing
All others who play music of their choosing.

And lit by a sudden artificial beam
A smocked pretender with his instrument,
Knowing that he is fragment of a dream,
Smirks none the less with borrowed merriment
And twangs for approbation from the front.

Why should they listen when he sings about
The joy of others that he cannot share?
A sexual gossip with a doll-like pout
He cannot touch the objects of his stare:
A prodigal's reflections swimming there.

The boy, his brother's hand upon his arm,
Sees neither where the lava flow of chance
Overtook habit, for he feels the palm
Of him whose turning muscle's nonchalance
Transforms to clockwork their prepared advance.

He too must pick an instrument at length
For this is painted during carnival:
Shall it be then a simple rung of strength
Or these with many strings where well-trained skill
May touch one while it keeps the others still?

And both must dress for the trooping, but the man
Is yet too active and the boy too young
For cloak or fur of heavy thought. They scan
The pace of silence, by the dancers shown
Robes of bright scarlet, horns that were never blown.

Rome

A Plan of Self-Subjection

A fragment of weak flesh that circles round
Between the sky and the hot crust of hell,
I circle because I have found
That tracing circles is a useful spell
Against contentment, which comes on by stealth;
Because I have found that from the heaven sun
Can scorch like hell itself,
I end my circle where I had begun.

I put this pen to paper and my verse
Imposes form upon my fault described
So that my fault is worse —
Not from condonement but from being bribed
With order: and with this it appears strong,
Which lacks all order that it can exist.
Yet before very long
From poem back to original I twist.

As Alexander or Mark Antony
Or Coriolanus, whom I most admire,
I mask self-flattery.
And yet however much I may aspire
I stay myself — no perfect king or lover
Or stoic. Even this becomes unreal.
Each tainted with the other
Becomes diseased, both self and self's ideal.

In sex do I not dither more than either
In verse or pose, does not the turncoat sense
Show itself slicker, lither
In changing sides according to the hints
That hopes give out, or action seems to breathe?
Here is most shade my longing, from the sun
And that hot hell beneath.
My circle's end is where I have begun.

Birthday Poem

You understand both Adolphe and Fabrice
   The speculative man or passionate;
You know the smarmies, but side-step the grease
   Ably appraising depth, direction, rate;
Through narrow seas you plunge, to seek the Fleece,
   So sure, you even risk arriving late,
   By flirting, hook-wise, with attractive bait.

You teach Adolphe a hair-raising escape
   Out of the round cell of his lover's eyes,
Show him a huge world with a violent shape;
   You teach Fabrice to sit and analyse;
The smart are dead waist-down: you wear no crêpe;
   You leave the mermaid, having formed no ties;
   You get the Golden Fleece, you are so wise.

Yet you for all the sanity and ease,
   The disconcerting smile omniscient,
Are prisoned in perplexity like these,
   Fabrice and Adolphe; on your discontent
An ailing parasite; to enemies,
   Ponces and whores, concede, because intent
   On groping round your own bewilderment.

First Meeting with a Possible Mother-in-Law

She thought, without the benefit of knowing,
You, who had been hers, were not any more.
We had locked our love in to leave nothing showing
From the room her handiwork had crammed before;
But – much revealing in its figured sewing –
A piece of stuff hung out, caught in the door.
I caused the same suspicion I watched growing:
Who could not tell what whole the part stood for?

There was small likeness between her and me:
Two strangers left upon a bare top landing,
I for a prudent while, she totally.

But, eyes turned from the bright material hint,
Each shared too long a second's understanding,
Learning the other's terms of banishment.

Autumn Chapter in a Novel

Through woods, Mme Une Telle, a trifle ill
With idleness, but no less beautiful,
Walks with the young tutor, round their feet
Mob syllables slurred to a fine complaint,
Which in their time held off the natural heat.

The sun is distant, and they fill out space
Sweatless as watercolour under glass.
He kicks abruptly. But we may suppose
The leaves he scatters thus will settle back
In much the same position as they rose.

A tutor's indignation works on air,
Altering nothing; action bustles where,
Towards the pool by which they lately stood,
The husband comes discussing with his bailiff
Poachers, the broken fences round the wood.

Pighead! The poacher is at large, and lingers,
A dead mouse gripped between his sensitive fingers:
Fences already keep the live game out:
See how your property twists her parasol,
Hesitates in the tender trap of doubt.

Here they repair, here daily handle lightly
The brief excitements that disturb them nightly;
Sap draws back inch by inch, and to the ground
The words they uttered rustle constantly:
Silent, they watch the growing, weightless mound.

They leave at last a chosen element,
Resume the motions of their discontent;
She takes her sewing up, and he again
Names to her son the deserts on the globe,
And leaves thrust violently upon the pane.

The Wheel of Fortune

Strapped helpless, monarchs and prelates, round they swung.
O mutability they cried, O perfect Wheel!
    The bishop dreamt of ruin while he dozed,
    A lover that his secrets were exposed,
And Lambert Simnel that he stirred the king's porridge.

Deeper they dream, disorder comes: high, low, are flung
Faster, limbs spinning. As the great Hub cracks they peel
    From off the Felloe of that even round.
    Bishop and lover sprawl upon the ground,
And Lambert Simnel stirs the under footman's porridge.

The Silver Age

Do not enquire from the centurion nodding
At the corner, with his head gentle over
The swelling breastplate, where true Rome is found.
Even of Livy there are volumes lost.
All he can do is guide you through the moonlight.

When he moves, mark how his eager striding,
To which we know the darkness is a river
Sullen with mud, is easy as on ground.
We know it is a river never crossed
By any but some few who hate the moonlight.

And when he speaks, mark how his ancient wording
Is hard with indignation of a lover.
'I do not think our new Emperor likes the sound
Of turning squadrons or the last post.
Consorts with Christians, I think he lives in moonlight.'

Hurrying to show you his companions guarding,
He grips your arm like a cold strap of leather,
Then halts, earthpale, as he stares round and round.
What made this one fragment of a sunken coast
Remain, far out, to be beaten by the moonlight?

The Unsettled Motorcyclist's Vision of his Death

Across the open countryside,
Into the walls of rain I ride.
It beats my cheek, drenches my knees,
But I am being what I please.

The firm heath stops, and marsh begins.
Now we're at war: whichever wins
My human will cannot submit
To nature, though brought out of it.
The wheels sink deep; the clear sound blurs:
Still, bent on the handle-bars,
I urge my chosen instrument
Against the mere embodiment.
The front wheel wedges fast between
Two shrubs of glazed insensate green
– Gigantic order in the rim
Of each flat leaf. Black eddies brim
Around my heel which, pressing deep,
Accelerates the waiting sleep.

I used to live in sound, and lacked
Knowledge of still or creeping fact,
But now the stagnant strips my breath,
Leant on my cheek in weight of death.
Though so oppressed I find I may
Through substance move. I pick my way,
Where death and life in one combine,
Through the dark earth that is not mine,
Crowded with fragments, blunt, unformed;
While past my ear where noises swarmed

The marsh plant's white extremities,
Slow without patience, spread at ease
Invulnerable and soft, extend
With a quiet grasping toward their end.

And though the tubers, once I rot,
Reflesh my bones with pallid knot,
Till swelling out my clothes they feign
This dummy is a man again,
It is as servants they insist,
Without volition that they twist;
And habit does not leave them tired,
By men laboriously acquired.
Cell after cell the plants convert
My special richness in the dirt:
All that they get, they get by chance.

And multiply in ignorance.

Lines for a Book

I think of all the toughs through history
And thank heaven they lived, continually.
I praise the overdogs from Alexander
To those who would not play with Stephen Spender.
Their pride exalted some, some overthrew,
But was not vanity at last: they knew
That though the mind has also got a place
It's not in marvelling at its mirrored face
And evident sensibility. It's better
To go and see your friend than write a letter;
To be a soldier than to be a cripple;
To take an early weaning from the nipple
Than think your mother is the only girl;
To be insensitive, to steel the will,
Than sit irresolute all day at stool
Inside the heart; and to despise the fool,
Who may not help himself and may not choose,
Than give him pity which he cannot use.
I think of those exclusive by their action,
For whom mere thought could be no satisfaction –
The athletes lying under tons of dirt
Or standing gelded so they cannot hurt
The pale curators and the families
By calling up disturbing images.
I think of all the toughs through history
And thank heaven they lived, continually.

Elvis Presley

Two minutes long it pitches through some bar:
Unreeling from a corner box, the sigh
Of this one, in his gangling finery
And crawling sideburns, wielding a guitar.

The limitations where he found success
Are ground on which he, panting, stretches out
In turn, promiscuously, by every note.
Our idiosyncrasy and our likeness.

We keep ourselves in touch with a mere dime:
Distorting hackneyed words in hackneyed songs
He turns revolt into a style, prolongs
The impulse to a habit of the time.

Whether he poses or is real, no cat
Bothers to say: the pose held is a stance,
Which, generation of the very chance
It wars on, may be posture for combat.

Market at Turk

At the street corner, hunched up,
he gestates action, prepared
for some unique combat in
boots, jeans, and a curious cap
whose very peak, jammed forward,
indicates resolution.

It is military, almost,
how he buckles himself in,
with bootstraps and Marine belt,
reminders of the will, lest
even with that hard discipline
the hardness should not be felt.

He waits, whom no door snatches
to unbuckling in the close
commotion of bar or bed,
he presides in apartness,
not yet knowing his purpose
fully, and fingers the blade.

In Praise of Cities

1

Indifferent to the indifference that conceived her,
Grown buxom in disorder now, she accepts
– Like dirt, strangers, or moss upon her churches –
Your tribute to the wharf of circumstance,
Rejected sidestreet, formal monument . . .
And, irresistible, the thoroughfare.

You welcome in her what remains of you;
And what is strange and what is incomplete
Compels a passion without understanding,
For all you cannot be.

2

Only at dawn
You might escape, she sleeps then for an hour:
Watch where she hardly breathes, spread out and cool,
Her pavements desolate in the dim dry air.

3

You stay. Yet she is occupied, apart.
Out of a mist the river turns to see
Whether you follow still. You stay. At evening
Your blood gains pace even as her blood does.

4

Casual yet urgent in her lovemaking,
She constantly asserts her independence:
Suddenly turning moist pale walls upon you
– Your own designs, peeling and unachieved –
Or her whole darkness hunching in an alley.
And all at once you enter the embrace
Withheld by day while you solicited.
She wanders lewdly, whispering her given name,
Charing Cross Road, or Forty-second Street:
The longest streets, desire that never ends,
Familiar and inexplicable, wearing
Cosmetic light a fool could penetrate.
She presses you with her hard ornaments,
Arcades, late movie shows, the piled lit windows
Of surplus stores. Here she is loveliest;
Extreme, material, and the work of man.

The Allegory of the Wolf Boy

The causes are in Time; only their issue
Is bodied in the flesh, the finite powers.
And how to guess he hides in that firm tissue
Seeds of division? At tennis and at tea
Upon the gentle lawn, he is not ours,
But plays us in a sad duplicity.

Tonight the boy, still boy open and blond,
Breaks from the house, wedges his clothes between
Two moulded garden urns, and goes beyond
His understanding, through the dark and dust:
Fields of sharp stubble, abandoned by machine
To the whirring enmity of insect lust.

As yet ungolden in the dense, hot night
The spikes enter his feet: he seeks the moon,
Which, with the touch of its infertile light,
Shall loose desires hoarded against his will
By the long urging of the afternoon.
Slowly the hard rim shifts above the hill.

White in the beam he stops, faces it square,
And the same instant leaping from the ground
Feels the familiar itch of close dark hair;
Then, clean exception to the natural laws,
Only to instinct and the moon being bound,
Drops on four feet. Yet he has bleeding paws.

Julian the Apostate

Lictor or heavy slave would wear it best,
The robe of uncapricious Emperor,
Waging a profitable war, at least
Knowing rule lay in gathered fold, not them.
But Julian bursts the doubly sacred hem;
Weighted enough by every growing hair.

Born in mid-progress of his history
He is perceptive of the sudden wrong
In those deliberate laws he framed today:
The absolute is hard to formulate:
Failure, desire, seek out their man; the date
Is relative, they die once they belong.

High in the palace, his concern is more
With a spirit self-created but cross-bred.
He sees them gather, reach the great church door,
Waving red flowers; from it frost: the bands
Of monks emerge with axes in their hands.
They swim among the pagans, white on red.

No subject can divert his cold resolve
To fix a question that, eluding name,
To make corporeal would be to solve.
The answer lies in some embodiment
Of question mark itself, not what is meant:
He stoops within that hypothetical frame.

Then strains to lift his bones erect, and fling
To the pure will of exclamation mark
In the discovered or discovering.
At length he pulls the only exclamation
Complete towards him, his assassination;
And greets an outrage of the simpler dark.

Jesus and his Mother

My only son, more God's than mine,
Stay in this garden ripe with pears.
The yielding of their substance wears
A modest and contented shine:
And when they weep with age, not brine
But lazy syrup are their tears.
'I am my own and not my own.'

He seemed much like another man,
That silent foreigner who trod
Outside my door with lily rod:
How could I know what I began
Meeting the eyes more furious than
The eyes of Joseph, those of God?
I was my own and not my own.

And who are these twelve labouring men?
I do not understand your words:
I taught you speech, we named the birds,
You marked their big migrations then
Like any child. So turn again
To silence from the place of crowds.
'I am my own and not my own.'

Why are you sullen when I speak?
Here are your tools, the saw and knife
And hammer on your bench. Your life
Is measured here in week and week
Planed as the furniture you make,
And I will teach you like a wife
To be my own and all my own.

Who like an arrogant wind blown
Where he may please, needs no content?
Yet I remember how you went
To speak with scholars in furred gown.
I hear an outcry in the town;
Who carried that dark instrument?
'One all his own and not his own.'

Treading the green and nimble sward
I stare at a strange shadow thrown.
Are you the boy I bore alone,
No doctor near to cut the cord?
I cannot reach to call you Lord,
Answer me as my only son.
'I am my own and not my own.'

St Martin and the Beggar

Martin sat young upon his bed
A budding cenobite,
Said, 'Though I hold the principles
Of Christian life be right,
I cannot grow from them alone,
I must go out to fight.'

He travelled hard, he travelled far,
The light began to fail.
'Is not this act of mine,' he said,
'A cowardly betrayal,
Should I not peg my nature down
With a religious nail?'

Wind scudded on the marshland,
And, dangling at his side,
His sword soon clattered under hail:
What could he do but ride? –
There was not shelter for a dog,
The garrison far ahead.

A ship that moves on darkness
He rode across the plain,
When a brawny beggar started up
Who pulled at his rein
And leant dripping with sweat and water
Upon the horse's mane.

He glared into Martin's eyes
With eyes more wild than bold;
His hair sent rivers down his spine;
Like a fowl plucked to be sold
His flesh was grey. Martin said –
'What, naked in this cold?

'I have no food to give you,
Money would be a joke.'
Pulling his new sword from the sheath
He took his soldier's cloak
And cut it in two equal parts
With a single stroke.

Grabbing one to his shoulders,
Pinning it with his chin,
The beggar dived into the dark,
And soaking to the skin
Martin went on slowly
Until he reached an inn.

One candle on the wooden table,
The food and drink were poor,
The woman hobbled off, he ate,
Then casually before
The table stood the beggar as
If he had used the door.

Now dry for hair and flesh had been
By warm airs fanned,
Still bare but round each muscled thigh
A single golden band,
His eyes now wild with love, he held
The half cloak in his hand.

'You recognised the human need
Included yours, because
You did not hesitate, my saint,
To cut your cloak across;
But never since that moment
Did you regret the loss.

'My enemies would have turned away,
My holy toadies would
Have given all the cloak and frozen
Conscious that they were good.
But you, being a saint of men,
Gave only what you could.'

St Martin stretched his hand out
To offer from his plate,
But the beggar vanished, thinking food
Like cloaks is needless weight.
Pondering on the matter,
St Martin bent and ate.

To Yvor Winters, 1955

I leave you in your garden.
                              In the yard
Behind it, run the Airedales you have reared
With boxer's vigilance and poet's rigour:
Dog-generations you have trained the vigour
That few can breed to train and fewer still
Control with the deliberate human will.
And in the house there rest, piled shelf on shelf,
The accumulations that compose the self –
Poem and history: for if we use
Words to maintain the actions that we choose,
Our words, with slow defining influence,
Stay to mark out our chosen lineaments.

Continual temptation waits on each
To renounce his empire over thought and speech,
Till he submit his passive faculties
To evening, come where no resistance is;
The unmotivated sadness of the air
Filling the human with his own despair.
Where now lies power to hold the evening back?
Implicit in the grey is total black:
Denial of the discriminating brain
Brings the neurotic vision, and the vein
Of necromancy. All as relative
For mind as for the sense, we have to live
In a half-world, not ours nor history's,
And learn the false from half-true premisses.

But sitting in the dusk – though shapes combine,
Vague mass replacing edge and flickering line,
You keep both Rule and Energy in view,
Much power in each, most in the balanced two:
Ferocity existing in the fence
Built by an exercised intelligence.
Though night is always close, complete negation
Ready to drop on wisdom and emotion,
Night from the air or the carnivorous breath,
Still it is right to know the force of death,
And, as you do, persistent, tough in will,
Raise from the excellent the better still.

The Inherited Estate

to Mike Kitay, an American in Europe

A mansion, string of cottages, a farm,
Before you reach the last black-timbered barn
And set your foot upon the path that leads
Up to the hill where Follies and façades
– Typical products of intelligence
That lacks brute purpose – split, disintegrate,
    And, falling with their own rich weight,
Litter the slopes, a record of expense.

So generations of the reckless dead
Put up the ruins you inherited,
And generations of ganged village boys
Have used as fort and ammunition those
Droppings of fashion you explore today.
What country boys and gentlemen have left
    Now smells of green, the fat dark drift
Where the weed's impulse couples with decay.

Is comfort so impermanently built,
A summer house with blurring fungus spilt
At random on the leaning walls? is time
Only a carved head that you fish from slime,
That winks with muddied eyeball? does the crash
Of failing stonework sound for all desires?
    For, once the dilettante tires,
The ornaments he raises fall in trash.

A calm discrimination marks your hate:
Once you inherited the wide estate
The Follies like the land and farm were yours.
Distance has flattered them, for from the moors
The fronts resembled solid palaces:
And though you are not so trusting to believe
    That all is sound which others leave,
You come not crediting half your bailiff says.

He told you all, an honest labourer.
But had not noticed this, that in the year
When you were born a twist of feckless wind
Brought one small seed and left it on the ground
Between the chance and choice to live or die.
It drew the means of living undeterred,
    Uncurling in the shell it stirred,
To rise, and sway upon your property.

Its art is merely holding to the earth –
But see how confidently, from its birth,
Its branches, lifting above failures, keep
Vigour within the discipline of shape.
Come here, friend, yearly, till you've carved the bark
With all the old virtues, young in fibre, names
    That swell with time and tree, no dreams,
No ornaments, but tallies for your work.

During an Absence

I used to think that obstacles to love
    Were out of date, the darkened stairs
Leading deprived ones to the mossy tomb
Where she lay carpeted with golden hairs:
    We had no place in such a room,
Belonging to the common ground above.

In sunlight we are free to move, and hold
    Our open assignations, yet
Each love defines its proper obstacles:
Our frowning Montague and Capulet
    Are air, not individuals
And have no faces for their frowns to fold.

Even in sunlight what does freedom mean?
    Romeo's passion rose to fire
From one thin spark within a brace of days.
We for whom time draws out, visas expire,
    Smoulder without a chance to blaze
Upon the unities of a paper scene.

The violence of a picturesque account
    Gives way to details, none the less
Reaching, each one more narrow than the last,
Down to a separate hygienic place
    Where acting love is in the past,
No golden hairs are there, no bleeding count.

No, if there were bright things to fasten on
    There'd be no likeness to the play.
But under a self-generated glare
Any bad end has possibility,
    The means endurance. I declare
I know how hard upon the ground it shone.

The Separation

Must we for ever eye through space? and make
Contact too much for comfort and yet less,
Like Peter Quint and that strange governess
Divided by a window or a lake?
Deprived like ghost, like man, both glare, then move
Apart in shadow. Must the breath swim between,
The trampled meadow of words yet intervene,
To part desire from the tall muscle of love?
I thought, that night, the evening of the tower,
When I could almost touch you, you were so clear,
That I was Quint and it was all the rest
Kept you away, the children or the hour;

But now you prowl in the garden and I am here,
What dead charge do I pull upon my breast?

High Fidelity

I play your furies back to me at night,
The needle dances in the grooves they made,
For fury is passion like love, and fury's bite,
These grooves, no sooner than a love mark fade;
Then all swings round to nightmare: from the rim,
To prove the guilt I don't admit by day,
I duck love as a witch to sink or swim
Till in the ringed and level I survey
The tuneless circles that succeed a voice.
They run, without distinction, passion, rage,
Around a soloist's merely printed name
That still turns, from the impetus not choice,
Surrounded in that played-out pose of age
By notes he was, but cannot be again.

Legal Reform

Condemned to life, a happier condemnation
Than I deserved, I serve my sentence full,
Clasping it to me at each indication
That this time love is not the paradox
By which, whatever it contains, my cell
Contains the absolute, because it locks.

It all led up to this, a simple law
Passed by ourselves, which holds me in its power.
Not till I stopped the theft of all I saw
Just for the having's sake, could it be passed.
Now I refer disposal of each hour
To this, a steady precedent at last.

My sentence stipulated exercise
Painful and lonely in the walks of death
With twittering clouds of spirits; still there lies
Beneath the common talk my single hope:
I must get back inside the cage of breath
For absence twitches on the loosened rope.

Marched off to happiness, I quarry stone
Hour after hour, and sweat my past away.
Already I have made, working alone,
Notable excavations, and the guard,
Turning desire, who eyes me all the day,
Has no use for his whip, I work so hard.

Condemned to hope, to happiness, to life,
Condemned to shift in your enclosing eyes,
I soon correct those former notions rife
Among the innocent, or fetter-maimed.
For law is in our hands, I realize:
The sentence is, condemned to be condemned.

Thoughts on Unpacking

Unpacking in the raw new rooms, I clear,
Or try to clear, a space for us, that we
May cultivate an ease of moving here
   With no encumbrance near,
In amplitude. But something hinders me:

Where do these go, these knick-knacks I forgot?
– Gadgets we bought and kept, thinking perhaps
They might be useful some day, and a lot
   Of others that were not:
Bent keys, Italian grammars, Mickey Mouse caps.

And there are worse grotesques that, out of sight,
Unpacked, unlabelled, somehow followed too:
The urgencies we did not share, the spite
   Of such and such a night,
Poses, mistakes – an unclean residue –

That drift, one after other, till I find
They have filled the space I carefully prepared;
The sagging shapes I thought we left behind
   Crawl out within the mind
Seeming to sneer 'This is the past you shared.'

I take a broom to them; but when I thrust
Round the diminished luggage, some roll back,
Surviving from my outbreak of disgust
   As balls of hair and dust
Made buoyant with a kind of fictive lack.

I need your help with these. They rest unseen
In furniture we know, and plot a changing
To grey confusion of the space between.
    Now, as I sweep it clean,
I realize that love is an arranging.

Merlin in the Cave: He Speculates without a Book

This was the end and yet, another start:
Held by the arms of lust from lust I pace
About the dim fulfilment of my art,
Impatient in the flesh I eye a space
Where, warlock, once I might have left this place,
A form of life my tool, creeping across
The shelving rock as rank convolvulus.

The Rock. The space, too narrow for a hand.
Pressing my head between two slopes of stone
I peer at what I do not understand,
The movement: clouds, and separate rooks blown
Back on their flight. Where do they fly, alone?
I lost their instinct. It was late. To me
The bird is only meat for augury.

And here the mauve convolvulus falls in,
Its narrow stalk as fat and rich in sap
As I was rich in lusting to begin
A life I could have had and finished up
Years, years before. With aphrodisiac
I brought back vigour; oiled and curled my hair;
Reduced my huge obesity, to wear

The green as tightly girdled at my waist
As any boy who leapt about the court;
And with an unguent I made my chest
Fit for the iron plate. I still held short
Of wrestling as the boys did: from their sport
They slid back panting on the tiles to look
At one distinguished now by scent, not book.

Love was a test: I was all-powerful,
So failed, because I let no fault intrude.
A philosophic appetite. By rule
I calculated each fond attitude
But those that self-distrust makes more than mood,
The quick illogical motions, negative
But evidence that lovers move and live.

I watch the flux I never guessed: the grass;
The watchful animal that gnaws a root,
Knowing possession means the risk of loss;
Ripeness that rests an hour in the fruit.
Yet locked here with the very absolute
I challenged, I must try to break the hold:
This cave is empty, and is very cold.

I must grow back through knowledge, passing it
Like casual landmarks in a well-known land,
Great mausoleums over ancient wit,
Doors that would swing at my complacent hand;
And come at last, being glad to understand
The touched, the seen, and only those, to where
I find the earth is suddenly black and near.

And having reached the point where there remain
No knacks or habits, and these empty cells
Are matched by a great emptiness in my brain:
Unhampered by remembered syllables,
The youth I wasted at precocious spells
Will grow upon me, and my wants agree
In the sweet promiscuity of the bee.

And yet, the danger. All within my mind
Hovers complete, and if it never grows
It never rots; for what I leave behind
Contains no fight within itself: the rose
Is full and drops no petal, emblems doze
Perfect and quiet as if engraved in books,
Not like the fighting boys and wind-torn rooks.

The bee's world and the rook's world are the same:
Where clouds do, or do not, let through the light;
Too mixed, unsimple, for a simple blame;
Belligerent: but no one starts the fight,
And nothing ends it but a storm or night.
Alchemists, only, boil away the pain,
And pick out value as one small dry grain.

And turned upon the flooding relative,
What could I do but start the quest once more
Towards the terrible cave in which I live,
The absolute prison where chance thrust me before
I built it round me on my study floor;
What could I do but seek the synthesis
As each man does, of what his nature is?

Knowing the end to movement, I will shrink
From movement not for its own wilful sake.
– How can a man live, and not act or think
Without an end? But I must act, and make
The meaning in each movement that I take.
Rook, bee, you are the whole and not a part.
This is an end, and yet another start.

The Corridor

A separate place between the thought and felt
The empty hotel corridor was dark.
But here the keyhole shone, a meaning spark.
What fires were latent in it! So he knelt.

Now, at the corridor's much lighter end,
A pierglass hung upon the wall and showed,
As by an easily deciphered code,
Dark, door, and man, hooped by a single band.

He squinted through the keyhole, and within
Surveyed an act of love that frank as air
He was too ugly for, or could not dare,
Or at a crucial moment thought a sin.

Pleasure was simple thus: he mastered it.
If once he acted as participant
He would be mastered, the inhabitant
Of someone else's world, mere shred to fit.

He moved himself to get a better look
And then it was he noticed in the glass
Two strange eyes in a fascinated face
That watched him like a picture in a book.

The instant drove simplicity away –
The scene was altered, it depended on
His kneeling, when he rose they were clean gone
The couple in the keyhole; this would stay.

For if the watcher of the watcher shown
There in the distant glass, should be watched too,
Who can be master, free of others; who
Can look around and say he is alone?

Moreover, who can know that what he sees
Is not distorted, that he is not seen
Distorted by a pierglass, curved and lean?
Those curious eyes, through him, were linked to these –

These lovers altered in the cornea's bend.
What could he do but leave the keyhole, rise,
Holding those eyes as equal in his eyes,
And go, one hand held out, to meet a friend?

Vox Humana

Being without quality
I appear to you at first
as an unkempt smudge, a blur,
an indefinite haze, mere-
ly pricking the eyes, almost
nothing. Yet you perceive me.

I have been always most close
when you had least resistance,
falling asleep, or in bars;
during the unscheduled hours,
though strangely without substance,
I hang, there and ominous.

Aha, sooner or later
you will have to name me, and,
as you name, I shall focus,
I shall become more precise.
O Master (for you command
in naming me, you prefer)!

I was, for Alexander,
the certain victory; I
was hemlock for Socrates;
and, in the dry night, Brutus
waking before Philippi
stopped me, crying out 'Caesar!'

Or if you call me the blur
that in fact I am, you shall
yourself remain blurred, hanging
like smoke indoors. For you bring,
to what you define now, all
there is, ever, of future.

My Sad Captains (1961)

The will is infinite and the execution confined,
the desire is boundless and the act a slave to limit.

Troilus and Cressida

In Santa Maria del Popolo

Waiting for when the sun an hour or less
Conveniently oblique makes visible
The painting on one wall of this recess
By Caravaggio, of the Roman School,
I see how shadow in the painting brims
With a real shadow, drowning all shapes out
But a dim horse's haunch and various limbs,
Until the very subject is in doubt.

But evening gives the act, beneath the horse
And one indifferent groom, I see him sprawl,
Foreshortened from the head, with hidden face,
Where he has fallen, Saul becoming Paul.
O wily painter, limiting the scene
From a cacophony of dusty forms
To the one convulsion, what is it you mean
In that wide gesture of the lifting arms?

No Ananias croons a mystery yet,
Casting the pain out under name of sin.
The painter saw what was, an alternate
Candour and secrecy inside the skin.
He painted, elsewhere, that firm insolent
Young whore in Venus' clothes, those pudgy cheats,
Those sharpers; and was strangled, as things went,
For money, by one such picked off the streets.

I turn, hardly enlightened, from the chapel
To the dim interior of the church instead,
In which there kneel already several people,
Mostly old women: each head closeted
In tiny fists holds comfort as it can.
Their poor arms are too tired for more than this
– For the large gesture of solitary man,
Resisting, by embracing, nothingness.

The Annihilation of Nothing

Nothing remained: Nothing, the wanton name
That nightly I rehearsed till led away
To a dark sleep, or sleep that held one dream.

In this a huge contagious absence lay,
More space than space, over the cloud and slime,
Defined but by the encroachments of its sway.

Stripped to indifference at the turns of time,
Whose end I knew, I woke without desire,
And welcomed zero as a paradigm.

But now it breaks – images burst with fire
Into the quiet sphere where I have bided,
Showing the landscape holding yet entire:

The power that I envisaged, that presided
Ultimate in its abstract devastations,
Is merely change, the atoms it divided

Complete, in ignorance, new combinations.
Only an infinite finitude I see
In those peculiar lovely variations.

It is despair that nothing cannot be
Flares in the mind and leaves a smoky mark
Of dread.
        Look upward. Neither firm nor free,

Purposeless matter hovers in the dark.

The Monster

I left my room at last, I walked
The streets of that decaying town,
I took the turn I had renounced
Where the carved cherub crumbled down.

Eager as to a granted wish
I hurried to the cul de sac.
Forestalled by whom? Before the house
I saw an unmoved waiting back.

How had she never vainly mentioned
This lover, too, unsatisfied?
Did she dismiss one every night?
I walked up slowly to his side.

Those eyes glazed like her windowpane,
That wide mouth ugly with despair,
Those arms held tight against the haunches,
Poised, but heavily staying there:

At once I knew him, gloating over
A grief defined and realized,
And living only for its sake.
It was myself I recognized.

I could not watch her window now,
Standing before this man of mine,
The constant one I had created
Lest the pure feeling should decline.

What if I were within the house,
Happier than the fact had been
– Would he, then, still be gazing here,
The man who never can get in?

Or would I, leaving at the dawn
A suppler love than he could guess,
Find him awake on my small bed,
Demanding still some bitterness?

Readings in French

I

Refining Mallarmé at last destroyed
Flesh, passion, and their consequent confusions;
His poetry continued in a void
Where only furniture could have illusions.

II

Though Edgar Poë writes a lucid prose,
Just and rhetorical without exertion,
It loses all lucidity, God knows,
In the single, poorly rendered English version.

III

Nothing Unusual about Marcel Proust
All are unmasked as perverts sooner or later,
With a notable exception – the narrator.

IV

L'Education sentimentale
Mme Arnoux is finely never there.
That is the point: the fineness, the despair.

V

Charles Baudelaire knew that the human heart
Associates with not the whole but part.
The parts are fetishes: invariable
Particularities which furnish hell.

From the Highest Camp

Nothing in this bright region melts or shifts.
The local names are concepts: the Ravine,
Pemmican Ridge, North Col, Death Camp, they mean
The streetless rise, the dazzling abstract drifts,
To which particular names adhere by chance,
From custom lightly, not from character.
We stand on a white terrace and confer;
This is the last camp of experience.

What is that sudden yelp upon the air?
And whose are these cold droppings? whose malformed
Purposeless tracks about the slope? We know.
The abominable endures, existing where
Nothing else can: it is – unfed, unwarmed –
Born of rejection, of the boundless snow.

Innocence

to Tony White

He ran the course and as he ran he grew,
And smelt his fragrance in the field. Already,
Running he knew the most he ever knew,
The egotism of a healthy body.

Ran into manhood, ignorant of the past:
Culture of guilt and guilt's vague heritage,
Self-pity and the soul; what he possessed
Was rich, potential, like the bud's tipped rage.

The Corps developed, it was plain to see,
Courage, endurance, loyalty and skill
To a morale firm as morality,
Hardening him to an instrument, until

The finitude of virtues that were there
Bodied within the swarthy uniform
A compact innocence, child-like and clear,
No doubt could penetrate, no act could harm.

When he stood near the Russian partisan
Being burned alive, he therefore could behold
The ribs wear gently through the darkening skin
And sicken only at the Northern cold,

Could watch the fat burn with a violet flame
And feel disgusted only at the smell,
And judge that all pain finishes the same
As melting quietly by his boots it fell.

Modes of Pleasure

I jump with terror seeing him,
Dredging the bar with that stiff glare
As fiercely as if each whim there
Were passion, whose passion is a whim:

The Fallen Rake, being fallen from
The heights of twenty to middle age,
And helpless to control his rage,
So mean, so few the chances come.

The very beauty of his prime
Was that the triumphs which recurred
In different rooms without a word
Would all be lost some time in time.

Thus he reduced the wild unknown.
And having used each hour of leisure
To learn by rote the modes of pleasure,
The sensual skills as skills alone,

He knows that nothing, not the most
Cunning or sweet, can hold him, still.
Living by habit of the will,
He cannot contemplate the past,

Cannot discriminate, condemned
To the sharpest passion of them all.
Rigid he sits: brave, terrible,
The will awaits its gradual end.

Modes of Pleasure

New face, strange face, for my unrest.
I hunt your look, and lust marks time
Dark in his doubtful uniform,
Preparing once more for the test.

You do not know you are observed:
Apart, contained, you wait on chance,
Or seem to, till your callous glance
Meets mine, as callous and reserved.

And as it does we recognize
That sharing an anticipation
Amounts to a collaboration –
A warm game for a warmer prize.

Yet when I've had you once or twice
I may not want you any more:
A single night is plenty for
Every magnanimous device.

Why should that matter? Why pretend
Love must accompany erection?
This is a momentary affection,
A curiosity bound to end,

Which as good-humoured muscle may
Against the muscle try its strength
– Exhausted into sleep at length –
And will not last long into day.

A Map of the City

I stand upon a hill and see
A luminous country under me,
Through which at two the drunk must weave;
The transient's pause, the sailor's leave.

I notice, looking down the hill,
Arms braced upon a window sill;
And on the web of fire escapes
Move the potential, the grey shapes.

I hold the city here, complete:
And every shape defined by light
Is mine, or corresponds to mine,
Some flickering or some steady shine.

This map is ground of my delight.
Between the limits, night by night,
I watch a malady's advance,
I recognize my love of chance.

By the recurrent lights I see
Endless potentiality,
The crowded, broken, and unfinished!
I would not have the risk diminished.

The Book of the Dead

The blood began to waste into the clods.
Meanwhile his soldiers kept the dead away
At sword-point, though some clamoured by the gods,
And some by friendship – hard, hard to deny.

Slowly the form took body; they could see
Blood flow down the diaphanous throat, slow, stay,
Clot, till the neck became opaque. And he,
Tiresias, stood before them, heavy as they.

What comfort could he bring them? (Circling past,
Poor, drained of cunning, they would also grope
After a goat's blood even.) Might the last
Action of which he spoke be ground for hope?
But winnowing is one action out of many.
After the winnowing, you must grind, bake, eat,
And then once more turn out into the rainy
Acres to plough, your mantle weighing wet
Round your swaddled ankles, your knuckles raw, your cheek
Fretted with tiny veins, – and not assured
That it will be, this time, either easier work
Or more successful. Even, perhaps, more hard.

Yet by the time Odysseus saw the throat,
Guttering, whiten, he was glad. The dead
Desire what they can never bring about;
The living bring discriminate gifts of blood,
Clumsily, wasting far more than they give,
But able still to bring. He knew the lack,
And watching, without comfort, was alive
Because he had no comfort. He turned back.

The Byrnies

The heroes paused upon the plain.
When one of them but swayed, ring mashed on ring:
   Sound of the byrnie's knitted chain,
Vague evocations of the constant Thing.

   They viewed beyond a salty hill
Barbaric forest, mesh of branch and root
    – A huge obstruction growing still,
Darkening the land, in quietness absolute.

   That dark was fearful – lack of presence –
Unless some man could chance upon or win
    Magical signs to stay the essence
Of the broad light that they adventured in.

   Elusive light of light that went
Flashing on water, edging round a mass,
    Inching across fat stems, or spent
Lay thin and shrunk among the bristling grass.

   Creeping from sense to craftier sense,
Acquisitive, and loss their only fear,
    These men had fashioned a defence
Against the nicker's snap, and hostile spear.

   Byrnie on byrnie! as they turned
They saw light trapped between the man-made joints,
    Central in every link it burned,
Reduced and steadied to a thousand points.

Thus for each blunt-faced ignorant one
The great grey rigid uniform combined
   Safety with virtue of the sun.
Thus concepts linked like chainmail in the mind.

   Reminded, by the grinding sound,
Of what they sought, and partly understood,
   They paused upon the open ground,
A little group above the foreign wood.

Black Jackets

In the silence that prolongs the span
Rawly of music when the record ends,
The red-haired boy who drove a van
In weekday overalls but, like his friends,

Wore cycle boots and jacket here
To suit the Sunday hangout he was in,
Heard, as he stretched back from his beer,
Leather creak softly round his neck and chin.

Before him, on a coal-black sleeve
Remote exertion had lined, scratched, and burned
Insignia that could not revive
The heroic fall or climb where they were earned.

On the other drinkers bent together,
Concocting selves for their impervious kit,
He saw it as no more than leather
Which, taut across the shoulders grown to it,

Sent through the dimness of a bar
As sudden and anonymous hints of light
As those that shipping give, that are
Now flickers in the Bay, now lost in night.

He stretched out like a cat, and rolled
The bitterish taste of beer upon his tongue,
And listened to a joke being told:
The present was the things he stayed among.

If it was only loss he wore,
He wore it to assert, with fierce devotion,
   Complicity and nothing more.
He recollected his initiation,

   And one especially of the rites.
For on his shoulders they had put tattoos:
   The group's name on the left, The Knights,
And on the right the slogan Born To Lose.

The Value of Gold

The hairs turn gold upon my thigh,
And I am gold beneath the sun,
Losing pale features that the cold
Pinched, pointed, for an instant I
Turn blind to features, being one
With all that has, like me, turned gold.

I finish up the can of beer,
And lay my head on the cropped grass:
Now bordering flag, geranium,
And mint-bush tower above me here,
Which colour into colour pass
Toward the last state they shall become.

Of insect size, I walk below
The red, green, greenish-black, and black,
And speculate. Can this quiet growth
Comprise at once the still-to-grow
And a full form without a lack?
And, if so, can I too be both?

I darken where perpetual
Action withdraws me from the sun.
Then from one high precocious stalk
A flower – its fulness reached – lets fall
Features, great petals, one by one
Shrivelling to gold across my walk.

Claus von Stauffenberg

of the bomb-plot on Hitler, 1944

What made the place a landscape of despair,
History stunned beneath, the emblems cracked?
Smell of approaching snow hangs on the air;
The frost meanwhile can be the only fact.

They chose the unknown, and the bounded terror,
As a corrective, who corrected live
Surveying without choice the bounding error:
An unsanctioned present must be primitive.

A few still have the vigour to deny
Fear is a natural state; their motives neither
Of doctrinaire, of turncoat, nor of spy.
Lucidity of thought draws them together.

The maimed young Colonel who can calculate
On two remaining fingers and a will,
Takes lessons from the past, to detonate
A bomb that Brutus rendered possible.

Over the maps a moment, face to face:
Across from Hitler, whose grey eyes have filled
A nation with the illogic of their gaze,
The rational man is poised, to break, to build.

And though he fails, honour personified
In a cold time where honour cannot grow,
He stiffens, like a statue, in mid-stride
— Falling toward history, and under snow.

2

I looked back as we crossed the crest of the
foothills – with the air so clear you could
see the leaves on Sunset Mountains two
miles away. It's startling to you sometimes
– just air, unobstructed, uncomplicated air.

F. Scott Fitzgerald, *The Last Tycoon*

Waking in a Newly Built House

The window, a wide pane in the bare
modern wall, is crossed by colourless
peeling trunks of the eucalyptus
recurring against raw sky-colour.

It wakes me, and my eyes rest on it,
sharpening, and seeking merely all
of what can be seen, the substantial,
where the things themselves are adequate.

So I observe them, able to see
them as they are, the neutral sections
of trunk, spare, solid, lacking at once
disconnectedness and unity.

There is a tangible remoteness
of the air about me, its clean chill
ordering every room of the hill-
top house, and convoking absences.

Calmly, perception rests on the things,
and is aware of them only in
their precise definition, their fine
lack of even potential meanings.

Flying Above California

Spread beneath me it lies – lean upland
sinewed and tawny in the sun, and

valley cool with mustard, or sweet with
loquat. I repeat under my breath

names of places I have not been to:
Crescent City, San Bernardino

– Mediterranean and Northern names.
Such richness can make you drunk. Sometimes

on fogless days by the Pacific,
there is a cold hard light without break

that reveals merely what is – no more
and no less. That limiting candour,

that accuracy of the beaches,
is part of the ultimate richness.

Considering the Snail

The snail pushes through a green
night, for the grass is heavy
with water and meets over
the bright path he makes, where rain
has darkened the earth's dark. He
moves in a wood of desire,

pale antlers barely stirring
as he hunts. I cannot tell
what power is at work, drenched there
with purpose, knowing nothing.
What is a snail's fury? All
I think is that if later

I parted the blades above
the tunnel and saw the thin
trail of broken white across
litter, I would never have
imagined the slow passion
to that deliberate progress.

'Blackie, the Electric Rembrandt'

We watch through the shop-front while
Blackie draws stars – an equal

concentration on his and
the youngster's faces. The hand

is steady and accurate;
but the boy does not see it

for his eyes follow the point
that touches (quick, dark movement!)

a virginal arm beneath
his rolled sleeve: he holds his breath.

. . . Now that it is finished, he
hands a few bills to Blackie

and leaves with a bandage on
his arm, under which gleam ten

stars, hanging in a blue thick
cluster. Now he is starlike.

Hotblood on Friday

Expectant yet relaxed, he
basks within the body's tight
limits, the tender reaches;
and acquires by street-light the
details which accumulate
to a sense of crude richness

that almost unseats reason.
At last, the present! His step
springs on the sidewalk like a
voice of appetite. The town
is gradually opening up,
this as on every Friday:

stone petals bright in the warm
evening. No hand can grasp it.
Quick, Hotblood, in the boisterous
community find some term,
precarious and accurate,
that assumes it without loss.

The Feel of Hands

The hands explore tentatively,
two small live entities whose shapes
I have to guess at. They touch me
all, with the light of fingertips

testing each surface of each thing
found, timid as kittens with it.
I connect them with amusing
hands I have shaken by daylight.

There is a sudden transition:
they plunge together in a full
formed single fury; they are grown
to cats, hunting without scruple;

they are expert but desperate.
I am in the dark. I wonder
when they grew up. It strikes me that
I do not know whose hands they are.

L'Epreuve

for Paul Bowles

1

My body trots semblably
on Market Street. I control
that thick and singular spy,
from a hovering planet: I
contemplate new laws meanwhile.

According to which it is
not a thoroughfare below
but a sweet compact. I choose
as if for the first time this
as the world I'll come back to.

2

Not yet. I am distinct. I
am now afflicted with thirst
heat and cold, bombarded by
rockets that explode greenly,
harried by shapes, cramped. The worst

is, I am still on my own.
The street's total is less near
during my long ordeal than
the turbanned legends within
my world of serried colour.

Rastignac at 45

Here he is of course. It was his best
trick always: when we glance again toward
the shadow we see it has consist-
ed of him all along, lean and bored.

We denounced him so often! Yet he
comes up, and leans on one of the bars
in his dark suit, indicating the
empty glass as if we were waiters.

We fill it, and submit, more or less,
to his marvellous air of knowing
all the ropes debonair weariness
could care to handle, of 'everything

that I know I know from having done,
child, and I survive.' What calmly told
confidences of exploration
among the oversexed and titled,

or request for a few days' loan, are
we about to hear? Rastignac tell
us about Life, and what men of your
stamp endure. It must be terrible.

It is. To the left of his mouth is
an attractive scarlike line, not caused
by time unhelped. It is not the prize,
either, of a dueller's lucky thrust.

But this: time after time the fetid
taste to the platitudes of Romance
has drawn his mouth up to the one side
secretly, in a half-maddened wince.

We cannot help but pity him that
momentary convulsion; however,
the mere custom of living with it
has, for him, diminished the horror.

Lights Among Redwood

And the streams here, ledge to ledge,
take care of light. Only to
the pale green ribs of young ferns
tangling above the creek's edge
it may sometimes escape, though
in quick diffusing patterns.

Elsewhere it has become tone,
pure and rarified; at most
a muted dimness coloured
with moss-green, charred grey, leaf-brown.
Calm shadow! Then we at last
remember to look upward:

constant, to laws of size and
age the thick forms hold, though gashed
through with Indian fires. At once
tone is forgotten: we stand
and stare – mindless, diminished –
at their rosy immanence.

of Muir Woods

Adolescence

After the history has been made,
and when Wallace's shaggy head

glares on London from a spike, when
the exiled general is again

gliding into Athens harbour
now as embittered foreigner,

when the lean creatures crawl out of
camps and in silence try to live;

I pass foundations of houses,
walking through the wet spring, my knees

drenched from high grass charged with water,
and am part, still, of the done war.

A Trucker

Sometimes it is like a beast
barely controlled by a man.
But the cabin is lofty
as a skull, and all the rest
extends from his foot as an
enormous throbbing body:

if he left anything to
chance – see his great frame capsize,
and his rubber limbs explode
whirling! and see there follow
a bright fountain of red eyes
tinkling sightless to the road.

Loot

1

I am approaching. Past dry
towers softly seeding from mere
delicacy of age, I
penetrate, through thickets, or

over warm herbs my feet press
to brief potency. Now with
the green quickness of grasses
mingles the smell of the earth,

raw and black. I am about
to raid the earth and open
again those low chambers that
wary fathers stand guard in.

2

Poised on hot walls I try to
imagine them caught beneath
in the village, in shadow:
I can almost hear them breathe.

This time what shall I take? Powers
hidden and agile, yield now
value: here, uniquely yours.
Direct me. But dark below

in the boneworks, you only
move in time with my pulse, and
observe without passion the
veer of my impassioned mind.

3
This. Hands numb from sifting soil
I find at last a trinket
carved whole from some mineral:
nameless and useless thing that

is for me to name and use.
But even as I relax my
fingers round its cool surface,
I am herald to tawny

warriors, woken from sleep, who
ride precipitantly down
with the blood toward my hands, through
me to retain possession.

My Sad Captains

One by one they appear in
the darkness: a few friends, and
a few with historical
names. How late they start to shine!
but before they fade they stand
perfectly embodied, all

the past lapping them like a
cloak of chaos. They were men
who, I thought, lived only to
renew the wasteful force they
spent with each hot convulsion.
They remind me, distant now.

True, they are not at rest yet,
but now that they are indeed
apart, winnowed from failures,
they withdraw to an orbit
and turn with disinterested
hard energy, like the stars.

Misanthropos (1965)

Misanthropos

to Tony Tanner and Don Doody

The Last Man

I

He avoids the momentous rhythm
of the sea, one hill suffices him
who has the entire world to choose from.

He melts through the brown and green silence
inspecting his traps, is lost in dense
thicket, or appears among great stones.

He builds no watch tower. He lives like
the birds, self-contained they hop and peck;
he could conceal himself for a week;

and he learns like them to keep movement
on the undipped wing of the present.
But sometimes when he wakes, with the print

of stone in his side, a relentless
memory of monstrous battle is
keener than counsel of the senses.

He opens, then, a disused channel
to the onset of hatred, until
the final man walks the final hill

without thought or feeling, as before.
If he preserves himself in nature,
it is as a lived caricature

of the race he happens to survive.
He is clothed in dirt. He lacks motive.
He is wholly representative.

2

At last my shout is answered! Are you near,
Man whom I cannot see but can hear?

Here.

The canyon hides you well, which well defended.
Sir, tell me, is the long war ended?

Ended.

I passed no human on my trip, a slow one.
Is it your luck, down there, to know one?

No one.

What have I left, who stood among mankind,
When the firm base is undermined?

A mind.

Yet, with a vacant landscape as its mirror,
What can it choose, to ease the terror?

Error.

Is there no feeling, then, that I can trust,
In spite of what we have discussed?

Disgust.

3

Earlier, travelling on the roads where grass
Softened the gutters for the marsh bird's nest,
He walked barefoot already, and already

His uniform was peeling from his back.
And coming to this hill across the plain,
He sloughed it bit by bit. Now that, alone,
He cannot seek himself as messenger,
Or bear dispatches between elm and oak,
It is a clumsy frock he starts to fashion
From skins of mole and rabbit; he considers
That one who wears it is without a role.
But the curled darling who survives the war
Has merely lost the admirers of those curls
That always lavished most warmth on his neck;
Though no one sees him, though it is the wind
Utters ambiguous orders from the plain,
Though nodding foxgloves are his only girls,
His poverty is a sort of uniform.
With a bone needle he pursues himself,
Stitching the patchwork spread across his lap,
A courier after identity, and sees
A pattern grow among the disarray.

4

The moon appears, distinct where all is dim,
    And steady in the orbit it must go.
    He lies in shadow, then light reaches him.
While, there! the Milky Way follows below,
    A luminous field that swings across the sky.
    The ancient rhythm almost comforts, slow
Bright mild recurrence that he might move by,
    Obedient in the act of breath, and lit,
    Mere life, by matter travelling sure and high.
But this is envy for the inanimate,
    The youth of things. On the dead globe he sees
    Markings as one might on the earth from it,

Where relics of emergent matter freeze.
  Down here, two more births followed on the first:
  Life, consciousness, like linked catastrophes.
Their sequence in him cannot be reversed
  Except in death, thus, when the features set.
  Meanwhile, he must live, as he looks, immersed
In consciousness that plots its own end yet;
  And since the plotter through success would lose
  Knowledge of it, he must without regret
Accept the inheritance he did not choose,
  As he accepted drafting for that war
  That was not of his choosing. He must use
The heaviness, the flaw, he always bore.
  The imperfect moon swims forward on its course;
  Yet, bathed by shade now, he imagines more –
  The clearest light in the whole universe.

5

Green overtaking green, it's
endless; squat grasses creep up,
briars cross, heavily weighed
branches overhang, thickets
crowd in on the brown earth gap
in green which is the path made

by his repeated tread, which,
enacting the wish to move,
is defined by avoidance
of loose ground, of rock and ditch,
of thorn-brimmed hollows, and of
poisoned beds. The ground hardens.

Bare within limits. The trick
is to stay free within them.
The path branches, branches still,
returning to itself, like
a discovering system,
or process made visible.

It rains. He climbs up the hill.
Drops are isolate on leaves,
big and clear. It is cool, and
he breathes the barbarous smell
of the wet earth. Nothing moves
at the edges of the mind.

Memoirs of the World
6

It has turned cold. I have been gathering wood,
Numb-fingered, hardly feeling what I touched,
Turning crisp leaves to pick up where I could
The damp sticks from beneath them. I have crouched
Piling them up to dry, all afternoon,
And have heard all afternoon, over and over,
Two falling notes – a sweet disconsolate tune,
As if the bird called, from its twiggy cover,
           Nót now, nót now, nót now.

I dislodge sticks for kindling, one by one,
From brambles. Struck by shade, I stand and see,
Half blinding me, the cold red setting sun
Through the meshed branches of a leafless tree.
It calls old sunsets to my mind, one most
Which coloured, similarly, the white-grey, blackened
Iron and slabbed concrete of a sentry post

With its cold orange. Let me live, one second,
Nót now, nót now, nót now.

Most poignant and most weakening, that recall.
Although I lived from day to day, too, there.
Yet the comparison makes me sensible
Of the diminishing warmth and light, which were,
Or seem to have been, diminished less than now.
The bird stops. Hardening in the single present,
I know, hearing wind rattle in a bough,
I have always harked thus after an incessant
Nót now, nót now, nót now.

7
Who was it in dark glasses?
Nobody in the street could
see if my eyes were open.
I took them off for movies
and sleep. I waited, I stood
an armed angel among men.

Between the dart of colours
I wore a darkening and
perceived an exact structure,
a chart of the world. The coarse
menace of line was deepened,
and light was slightly impure.

Yet as I lingered there was,
I noticed, continual
and faint, an indecision,
a hunger in the senses.
I would devour the thin wail
of foghorns, or abandon

my whole self time after time
to the chipped glossy surface
of some doorjamb, for instance,
cramming my nail with its grime,
stroking humps where colourless
paint had filled faults to substance.

I was presence without full
being: from the streetcorner,
in the mere fact of movement,
was I entering the role
of spy or spied on, master
or the world's abject servant?

8

Dryads, reposing in the bark's hard silence,
Circled about the edges of my fire,
Exact in being, absolute in balance,
Instruct me how to find here my desire:

To separate the matter from its burning,
Where, in the flux that your composures lack,
Each into other constantly is turning.
In the glowing fall of ash – rose, grey, and black,

I search for meaning, studying to remember
What the world was, and meant. Therefore I try
To reconstruct it in a dying ember,
And wonder, does fire make it live or die?

And evil everywhere or nowhere, stealing
Out of my reach, on air, shows like a spark.
I think I grasp it. The momentary feeling
Is merely pain, evil's external mark.

The neighbouring cinders redden now together,
Like earlier worlds to search, where I am shown
Only myself, although I seek another,
A man who burnt from sympathy alone.

9

A serving man. Curled my hair,
wore gloves in my cap. I served
all degrees and both sexes.
But I gave readily from
the largess of high spirits,
a sturdy body and strong

fingers. Nor was I servile.
No passer-by could resist
the fragrant impulse nodding
upon my smile. I laboured
to become a god of charm,
an untirable giver.

Needing me, needing me, 'Quick!'
they would call: I came gladly.
Even as I served them sweets
I served myself a trencher
of human flesh in some dark
sour pantry, and munched from it.

My diet, now, is berries,
water, and the gristle of
rodents. I brought myself here,
widening the solitude
till it was absolute. But
at times I am ravenous.

10

All that snow pains my eyes, but I stare
on, stare on, lying in my shelter,

feverish, out at the emptiness.
A negative of matter, it is

a dead white surface at random crossed
by thin twigs and bird tracks on the crust

like fragments of black netting: hard, cold,
windswept. But now my mind loses hold

and, servant to an unhinged body,
becoming of it, sinks rapidly

beneath the stitched furs I'm swaddled in,
beneath the stink of my trembling skin,

[141]

till it enters the heart of fever,
as its captive, unable to stir.

I watch the cells swimming in concert
like nebulae, calm, without effort,

great clear globes, pink and white. – But look at
the intruder with blurred outline that

glides in among the shoals, colourless,
with tendrils like an anemone's

drifting all around it like long fur,
gently, unintelligently. Where

it touches it holds, in an act of
enfolding, possessing, merging love.

There is coupling where no such should be.
Surely it is a devil, surely

it is life's parody I see, which
enthralls a universe with its rich

heavy passion, leaving behind it
gorgeous mutations only, then night.

It ends. I open my eyes to snow.
I can sleep now; as I drowse I know

I must keep to the world's bare surface,
I must perceive, and perceive what is:

for though the hold of perception must
harden but diminish, like the frost,

yet still there may be something retained
against the inevitable end.

II

Epitaph for Anton Schmidt

The Schmidts obeyed, and marched on Poland.
And there an Anton Schmidt, Feldwebel,
Performed uncommon things, not safe,
Nor glamorous, nor profitable.

Was the expression on his face
'Reposeful and humane good nature'?
Or did he look like any Schmidt,
Of slow and undisclosing feature?

I know he had unusual eyes,
Whose power no orders might determine,
Not to mistake the men he saw,
As others did, for gods or vermin.

For five months, till his execution,
Aware that action has its dangers,
He helped the Jews to get away
— Another race at that, and strangers.

He never did mistake for bondage
The military job, the chances,
The limits; he did not submit
To the blackmail of his circumstances.

I see him in the Polish snow,
His muddy wrappings small protection,
Breathing the cold air of his freedom
And treading a distinct direction.

Elegy on the Dust

12

The upper slopes are busy with the cricket;
   But downhill, hidden in the thicket,
Birds alternate with sudden piercing calls
   The rustling from small animals
Retreating, venturing, as they hunt and breed
   Interdependent in that shade.

Beneath it, glare and silence cow the brain
   Where, troughed between the hill and plain,
The expanse of dust waits: acres calm and deep,
   Swathes folded on themselves in sleep
Or waves that, as if frozen in mid-roll,
   Hang in ridged rows. They cannot fall,
Yet imperceptibly they shift, at flood,
   In quiet encroachment on the wood –
First touching stalk and leaf with silvery cast,
   They block the pores to death at last
And drift in silky banks around the trunk,
   Where dock and fern are fathoms sunk.

Yet farther from the hill the bowl of dust
    Is open to the casual gust
That dives upon its silence, teasing it
    Into a spasm of wild grit.
Here it lies unprotected from the plain,
    And vexed with constant loss and gain,
It seems, of the world's refuse and debris,
    Turns to a vaguely heaving sea,
Where its own eddies, spouts, and calms appear.
    But seas contain a graveyard: here
The graveyard is the sea, material things
    – From stone to claw, scale, pelt, and wings –
Are all reduced to one form and one size.
    And here the human race, too, lies.
An imperfection endlessly refined
    By the imperfection of the mind.
They have all come who sought distinction hard
    To this universal knacker's yard,
Blood dried, flesh shrivelled, and bone decimated:
    Motion of life is thus repeated,
A process ultimately without pain
    As they are broken down again.
The remnants of their guilt mix as they must
    And average out in grains of dust
Too light to act, too small to harm, too fine
    To simper or betray or whine.

Each colourless hard grain is now distinct,
    In no way to its neighbour linked,
Yet from wind's unpremeditated labours
    It drifts in concord with its neighbours,
Perfect community in its behaviour.
    It yields to what it sought, a saviour:

Scattered and gathered, irregularly blown,
   Now sheltered by a ridge or stone,
Now lifted on strong upper winds, and hurled
   In endless hurry round the world.

The First Man

13

The present is a secure place to inhabit,
The past being fallen from the mind, the future
A repetition, only, with variations:
The same mouse on its haunches, nibbling, absorbed,
Another piece of root between the forefeet
Slender as wishbones; the woodlice, silvery balls;
The leaves still falling in vestiges of light.

Is he a man? If man is cogitation,
This is at most a rudimentary man,
An unreflecting organ of perception;
Slow as a bull, in moving; yet, in taking,
Quick as an adder. He does not dream at night.

Echo is in the past, the snow long past,
The year has recovered and put forth many times.

He is bent, looks smaller, and is furred, it seems.
Molelike he crouches over mounds of dirt,
Sifting. His eyes have sunk behind huge brows.
His nostrils twitch, distinguishing one by one
The smells of the unseen that blend to make
The black smell of the earth, smell of the Mother,
Smell of her food: pale tender smell of worms,
Tough sweet smell of her roots. He is a nose.
He picks through the turned earth, and eats. A mouth.

If he is man, he is the first man lurking
In a thicket of time. The mesh of green grows tighter.
There is yew, and oak picked out with mistletoe.
Watch, he is darkening in the heavy shade
Of trunks that thicken in the ivy's grip.

14

   'What is it? What?'
Mouth struggles with the words that mind forgot.
   While from the high brown swell
He watches it, the smudge, he sees it grow
As it crawls closer, crawls unturnable
And unforeseen upon the plain below.

   'That must be men.'
Knowledge invades him, yet he shrinks again
   And sickens to live still
Upon the green slopes of his isolation,
The 'final man upon a final hill,'
As if he did a sort of expiation.

   And now he dreams
Of a shadowed pool nearby fed by two streams:
   If he washed there, he might,
Skin tautened from the chill, emerge above,
Inhuman as a star, as cold, as white,
Freed from all dust. And yet he does not move.

   Could he assert
To men who climb up in their journey's dirt
   That clean was separate?

The dirt would dry back, hardening in the heat:
Perpetual that unease, that world of grit
Breathed in, and gathered on the hands and feet.

He is unaware
Of the change already taking place as there,
In the cold clear early light
He, lingering on the scorched grass wet with dew,
Still hunched but now a little more upright,
In picturing man almost becomes man too.

15

Hidden behind a rock, he watches, grown
As stony as a lizard poised on stone.
Below, the indeterminate shape flows steady
From plain to wood, from wood to slope. Already
Sharp outlines break, in movement, from the edge.
Then in approach upon the final ridge
It is slowly lost to sight, but he can hear
The shingle move with feet. Then they appear,
Being forty men and women, twos and threes,
Over the rim. From where he is he sees
One of the last men stumble, separate,
Up to the rock, this rock, and lean on it.
You can hear him gulp for wind, he is so close,
You can hear his hand rasp on the shrivelled moss
Blotching the rock: by peering you can see
What a ribbed bony creature it must be,
Sweat streaking dirt at collarbones and spine,
Sores round the mouth disfiguring the line.

And on the thin chest two long parallel
Clear curving scratches are discernible.
Recent, for only now the drops within
Steal through the white torn edges of the skin
To mix with dirt. Round here, such cuts are common.
It is not hard to visualize the human,
Tired, walking upward on a wooded slant;
Keeping his eyes upon the ground in front,
He made his way round some dropped rotten limb,
And a hanging briar unnoticed swung at him.
And only later does it start to sting.
That wood has its own way of countering.
The watcher is disturbed, not knowing why.
He has with obstinate equanimity,
Unmoving and unmoved, watched all the rest,
But seeing the trivial scratches on the chest,
He frowns. And he performs an action next
So unconsidered that he is perplexed,
Even in performing it, by what it means –
He walks around to where the creature leans.
The creature sees him, jumps back, staggers, calls,
Then, losing balance on the pebbles, falls.

Now that he has moved toward, through, and beyond
The impulse he does not yet understand,
He must continue where he has begun,
Finding, as when a cloud slips from the sun,
He has entered, without stirring, on a field
The same and yet more green and more detailed,
Each act of growth discovered by his gaze;
Yet if the place is changed by what surveys,
He is surveyed and he himself is changed,
Bombarded by perceptions, rearranged –

Rays on the skin investing with a shape,
A clarity he cannot well escape.

He stops, bewildered by his force, and then
Lifts up the other to his feet again.

16

Others approach, and I grip
his arm. For it seems to me
they file past my mind, my mind
perched on this bare rock, watching.

They turn and look at me full,
and as they pass they name me.

What is the name Adam speaks
after the schedule of beasts?

Though I grip his arm, the man,
the scratched man, seems among them,
and as he pauses the old
bitter dizziness hits me:
I almost fall. The stale stench!
the hangdog eyes, the pursed mouth!
no hero or saint, that one.

It is a bare world, and lacks
history; I am neither
his lord nor his servant.

By an act of memory,
I make the recognition:
I stretch out the word to him
from which conversations start,
naming him, also, by name.

17

Others approach. Well, this one may show trust
   Around whose arm his fingers fit.
The touched arm feels of dust, mixing with dust
     On the hand that touches it.

And yet a path is dust, or it is none,
  – Merely unstable mud, or weeds,
Or a stream that quietly slips on and on
     Through the undergrowth it feeds.

His own flesh, which he hardly feels, feels dust
   Raised by the war both partly caused
And partly fought, and yet survived. You must,
     If you can, pause; and, paused,

Turn out toward others, meeting their look at full,
   Until you have completely stared
On all there is to see. Immeasurable,
     The dust yet to be shared.

Poems from the 1960s

The Goddess

When eyeless fish meet her on
her way upward, they gently
turn together in the dark
brooks. But naked and searching
as a wind, she will allow
no hindrance, none, and bursts up

through potholes and narrow flues
seeking an outlet. Unslowed
by fire, rock, water or clay,
she after a time reaches
the soft abundant soil, which
still does not dissipate her

force – for look! sinewy thyme
reeking in the sunlight; rats
breeding, breeding, in their nests;
and the soldier by a park
bench with his greatcoat collar
up, waiting all evening for

a woman, any woman
her dress tight across her ass
as bark in moonlight. Goddess,
Proserpina: it is we,
vulnerable, quivering,
who stay you to abundance.

The Kiss at Bayreuth

Colours drain, shapes blur, resisting,
details swim together, the mass
of the external wobbles, sways,
disintegrating, yet seems to
hesitate before it is sucked
into the eye of the cyclone.

What is this pillar with the eye
that bares and discolours the world,
surrounded by the wash of time?
The inhuman eye contemplates
its own calm inclusive fulness,
its tendency, even, toward death.

The two, their turbulence the kiss
and yet annulled by it, may then
be said to both move and be still,
move in awareness and be still,
to, for one moment and only
that moment, not think of themselves.

Berlin in Ruins

Anhalter Bahnhof

It has an edge, or many edges.
The memory that most recurs is
of bronze Imperial fantasies

squirming with plump hauteur on the one
wall of a brown-brick railway station
soon to be reduced. That great ruin

totters beneath associations.
But you encounter a resistance,
and yourself resist. It is at once

unyielding in texture and fertile.
The mind does not rest without peril
among the tarnished blades of laurel:

it may cut on them, it may fester
– until it throbs with a revived fear
of the dark hysteric conqueror

returning from France in triumph as
the hectic that overtakes process,
beneath a silk tent of swastikas.

And fever may descend on the brow
like the high circlet, in whose shadow
the mind awakes, bathed in poison now;

or, harder and sharper than bronze, still
supporting the insupportable,
it may survive its own stiff laurel.

Confessions of the Life Artist

1

Whatever is here, it is
material for my art.

On the extreme shore of land,
and facing the disordered
rhythms of the sea, I taste
a summoning on the air.

I derive from these rocks, which
inhibit the sea's impulse.
But it is a condition,
once accepted, like air: air
haunted by the taste of salt.

2

I think, therefore I cannot
avoid thought of the morrow.
Outside the window, the birds
of the air and the lily
have lost themselves in action.
I think of the birds that sleep
in flight, of the lily's pale
waxy gleaming, of myself,
and of the morrow pending.
The one thing clear is that I
must not lose myself in thought.

3

You control what you can, and
use what you cannot.

                    Heady,
to hover above the winds,
buoyant with a sense of choice.
Circling over a city,
to reject the thousand, and
to select the one. To watch
the goodly people there, to
know that their blood circulates,
that it races as yours does,
live between extremities.

4

But what of the unchosen?

They are as if dead. Their deaths,
now, validate the chosen.

Of course, being left as dead
may lead to the thing itself.
I read about them: and what
could be more fortifying
to one's own identity
than another's suicide?

If there are forbidden arts,
mine must indeed be of them.

5

She is immersed in despair,
but I am here, luckily.
She, become indefinite,
leans on me who am starkly
redefined at each moment,
aware of her need, and trained
to have few needs of my own.

As I support her, so, with
my magnificent control,
I suddenly ask: 'What if
she has the edge over me?'

6

To give way to all passions,
I know, is merely whoring.
Yes, but to give way to none
is to be a whore-master.

I stride through the whore-house
when my girls are off duty,
I load them with chocolates,
but cannot for one moment
possess red hair like hers, fresh
cheeks or bee-stung lips like hers,
or a wasteful heart like hers.

7

I elevate not what I
have, but what I wish to have,
and see myself in others.

There is a girl in the train
who emulates the bee-hive
of the magazine stars of
four years ago.
                        I blush at
the jibes that grow inside me,
lest someone should utter them.

Why was something evolved so
tender, so open to pain?

8

Here is a famous picture.

It is of a little Jew
in Warsaw, some years ago,
being hustled somewhere. His
mother dressed him that morning
warmly in cap and cloth coat.
He stares at the camera
as he passes. Whatever
those big shining dark eyes have
just looked on, they can see now
no appeal in the wide world.

9

I grow old in the design.

Prophecies become fulfilled,
though never as expected,
almost accidentally,
in fact, as if to conform
to some alien order.

But I am concerned with my
own knowledge that the design
is everywhere ethical
and harmonious: circles
start to close, lines to balance.

10

The art of designing life
is no excuse for that life.

People will forget Shakespeare.
He will lie with George Formby
and me, here where the swine root.
Later, the solar system
will flare up and fall into
space, irretrievably lost.

For the loss, as for the life,
there will be no excuse, there
is no justification.

No Speech from the Scaffold

There will be no speech from
the scaffold, the scene must
be its own commentary.

The glossy chipped
surface of the block is like
something for kitchen use.

And the masked man with his
chopper: we know him: he
works in a warehouse nearby.

Last, the prisoner, he
is pale, he walks through
the dewy grass, nodding

a goodbye to acquaintances.
There will be no speech. And we
have forgotten his offence.

What he did is, now,
immaterial. It is the
execution that matters, or,

rather, it is his conduct
as he rests there, while
he is still a human.

Taylor Street

The small porch of imitation
marble is never sunny, but
outside the front door he
sits on his kitchen chair facing
the street. In the bent yellowish
face, from under the brim
of a floppy brown hat,
his small eyes watch what
he is not living. But he
lives what he can:
watches without a smile, with
a certain strain, the warmth
of his big crumpled
body anxiously cupped
by himself in himself, as
he leans over himself not
over the cold railing, un-
moving but carefully getting
a little strength from the sight of the
passers-by. He has it
all planned: he will live
here morning by morning.

The Conversation of Old Men

He feels a breeze rise from
the Thames, as far off
as Rotherhithe, in
intimate contact with
water, slimy hulls,
dark wood greenish
at waterline – touching
then leaving what it
lightly touches; he
goes on talking, and this is
the life of wind on water.

The Old Woman

Something approaches, about
which she has heard a good deal.
Her deaf ears have caught it, like
a silence in the wainscot
by her head. Her flesh has felt
a chill in her feet, a draught
in her groin. She has watched it
like moonlight on the frayed wood
stealing toward her
floorboard by floorboard. Will it hurt?

Let it come, it is
the terror of full repose,
and so no terror.

Touch

You are already
asleep. I lower
myself in next to
you, my skin slightly
numb with the restraint
of habits, the patina of
self, the black frost
of outsideness, so that even
unclothed it is
a resilient chilly
hardness, a superficially
malleable, dead
rubbery texture.

You are a mound
of bedclothes, where the cat
in sleep braces
its paws against your
calf through the blankets,
and kneads each paw in turn.

Meanwhile and slowly
I feel a is it
my own warmth surfacing or
the ferment of your whole
body that in darkness beneath
the cover is stealing
bit by bit to break
down that chill.

You turn and
hold me tightly, do
you know who
I am or am I
your mother or
the nearest human being to
hold on to in a
dreamed pogrom.

What I, now loosened,
sink into is an old
big place, it is
there already, for
you are already
there, and the cat
got there before you, yet
it is hard to locate.
What is more, the place is
not found but seeps
from our touch in
continuous creation, dark
enclosing cocoon round
ourselves alone, dark
wide realm where we
walk with everyone.

The Vigil of Corpus Christi

Swaddled to his nose against the chill
he stood all night, like a sentinel
at limits, by the pitted stone wall.

His body was scattered; each grease clot,
each lump and fold in the stiff blanket,
the aches, the circle of his wide hat

touched him at unrelated edges.
But perched above the blanket, his eyes
persisted, trying to become as

steadfast as the dark confronting them.
Then the sky paled: night relinquished him,
like seas casting him up whole through foam.

A footbath clattered in the distance;
his dog ran up and licked him. Each sense
tested itself, sharp from abeyance.

Was this, then, the end of any quest?
the invasion of himself at last
merely by himself? 'To be steadfast,'

he breathed: like a soldier, he straightened.
But the moist tongue went on working round
his ankles; and then, slowly, he grinned

with an unsoldierly joy, at this
soft sweet power awake in his own mass
balanced on his two feet, this fulness.

From an Asian Tent

Alexander thinks of his father

Father, I scarcely could believe you dead.
The pelts, fur trophies, and hacked skulls that you
Drunkenly hooked up while the bone still bled
I pulled down, and I hung the place instead
With emblems of an airy Hellene blue.

You held me once before the army's eyes;
During their endless shout, I tired and slid
Down past your forearms to the cold surprise
Your plated shoulder made between my thighs.
This happened. Or perhaps I wish it did.

Remembering that you never reached the East,
I have made it mine to the obscurest temple;
Yet each year look more like the man I least
Choose to resemble, bully, drunk, and beast.
Are you a warning, Father, or an example?

In the Tank

A man sat in the felon's tank, alone,
Fearful, ungrateful, in a cell for two.
And from his metal bunk, the lower one,
He studied where he was, as felons do.

The cell was clean and cornered, and contained
A bowl, grey gritty soap, and paper towels,
A mattress lumpy and not over-stained,
Also a toilet, for the felon's bowels.

He could see clearly all there was to see,
And later when the lights flicked off at nine
He saw as clearly all there was to see:
An order without colour, bulk, or line.

And then he knew exactly where he sat.
For though the total riches could not fail
– Red weathered brick, fountains, wisteria – yet
Still they contained the silence of a jail,

The jail contained a tank, the tank contained
A box, a mere suspension, at the centre,
Where there was nothing left to understand,
And where he must re-enter and re-enter.

The Clock

The room is like a cave, the webs of night
    Warm from a creature's sleep, that stir,
    But gently, from the draught and light
I bring in with me through the opening door.

I sense a creature, as if breathing came
    Through currents of minute packed life;
    It is not from the pilot-flame
Lifting its pallor like a blameless wife.

And, as I take the latch-key from the lock,
    I turn round listening – there it is,
    Its white-green twelve eyes fixed, the clock,
Prim compact monster of the silences.

That ticking dominates the other sounds,
    Slight creakings, flurries, and small sighs,
    As it continues on its rounds
Disposing of the world without surprise.

Indifferent to the accidents of a house,
    The ashes sifting from a grate,
    The spider's tread, the hurrying mouse,
The arguments of love sickening to hate.

Such is its mercy. In the winter cave,
    I wait upon the dark, I sit
    Fearing the monster that I crave,
Fearing the mercy and the need for it.

Back to Life

Around the little park
The lamps blink on, and make the dusk seem deeper.
I saunter toward them on the grass
That suddenly rustles from the dew,
Hearing behind, at times,
A fragmentary shout or distant bark.
I am alone, like a patrolling keeper.
And then I catch the smell of limes
Coming and going faintly on the dark:
Bunched black at equal height
They stand between the lamps, yet where
They branch out toward them on each side, a few
Touching the lighted glass,
Their leaves are soft green on the night,
The closest losing even their mass,
Edged but transparent as if they too gave light.

The street is full, the quiet is broken.
I notice that the other strollers there
Extend themselves, at ease
As if just woken
To a world they have not yet recovered, though
They move across the dusk, alert,
And stare,
As I do, into shops or at the trees,
Devouring each detail, from leaf to dirt,
In the measured mildness of the air.
Here by the kerb
The boys and girls walk, jostling as they grow,
Cocky with surplus strength.

And weakening with each move, the old,
Cushioned with papers or with rugs
On public seats close by,
Inch down into their loosened flesh, each fold
Being sensible of the gravity
Which tugs
And longs to bring it down
And break its hold.

I walk between the kerb and bench
Conscious at length
Of sharing through each sense,
As if the light revealed us all
Sustained in delicate difference
Yet firmly growing from a single branch.

If that were all of it!
The branch that we grow on
Is not remembered easily in the dark,
Or the transparency when light is gone:
At most, a recollection
In the mind only – over a rainswept park
Held to by mere conviction
In cold and misery when the clock strikes one.

The lamp still shines.
The pale leaves shift a bit,
Now light, now shadowed, and their movement shared
A second later by the bough,
Even by the sap that runs through it:
A small full trembling through it now
As if each leaf were, so, better prepared
For falling sooner or later separate.

Pierce Street

Nobody home. Long threads of sunlight slant
Past curtains, blind, and slat, through the warm room.
The beams are dazzling, but, random and scant,
Pierce where they end
                         small areas of the gloom
On curve of chair leg or a green stalk's bend.

I start exploring. Beds and canvases
Are shapes in each room off the corridor,
Their colours muted, square thick presences
Rising between
                    the ceiling and the floor,
A furniture inferred much more than seen.

Here in the seventh room my search is done.
A bluefly circles, irregular and faint.
And round the wall above me friezes run:
Fixed figures drawn
                    in charcoal or in paint.
Out of night now the flesh-tint starts to dawn.

Some stand there as if muffled from the cold,
Some naked in it, the wind around a roof.
But armed, their holsters as if tipped with gold.
And twice life-size –
                  in line, in groups, aloof,
They all stare down with large abstracted eyes.

A silent garrison, and always there,
They are the soldiers of the imagination
Produced by it to guard it everywhere.
Bodied within

        the limits of their station
As, also, I am bodied in my skin,

They vigilantly preserve as they prevent
And are the thing they guard, having some time stood
Where the painter reached to make them permanent.
The floorboards creak.

        The house smells of its wood.
Those who are transitory can move and speak.

Aqueduct

A dribble lights a shelf
That throats the aqueduct:
Inch like a glaze of salt.
And green, there, seeks itself,
A moss-film that has sucked
From seepings of the fault.

Later, a crop appears —
First shoots that sunlight pulls,
Then green blooms, then at last
The feathery seeded ears
Fine as the tentacles
Of earth fleas hopping past:

Till brilliant mottled patches
Invest the inch of stone
And ripen toward their gold;
And crops that no one watches
Seasonally resown
Extend the small tight hold.

Earth waited through its prime
For this, the smallest crack
By which the construct yields,
And draws it into time
By fleshing the attack
With green and golden fields.

The Inside-Outside Game

Outside, to corpse and fish, means atmosphere.
A roof is the stars' floor. That man's still here –
Outside the room but still inside the house;
    Only its hole is inside to the mouse.

Out of your skull, you look down dizzying,
On that bone-dovetailed, domed protecting thing.
Funny at first, the game. After a bit
    I was scared shitless at the thought of it.

I saw the world's nerves, then I turned about
To see myself, uncreased and inside out.
Look, look: rose tracing and bone imprint bare,
    Raw to the air's blade. And I touched the air.

Moly (1971)

When I was near the house of Circe, I met Hermes in the likeness of a young man, the down just showing on his face. He came up to me and took my hand, saying: 'Where are you going, alone, and ignorant of the way? Your men are shut up in Circe's sties, like wild boars in their lairs. But take heart, I will protect you and help you. Here is a herb, one of great virtue: keep it about you when you go to Circe's house.' As he spoke he pulled the herb out of the ground and showed it to me. The root was black, the flower was as white as milk; the gods call it Moly.

Rites of Passage

Something is taking place.
Horns bud bright in my hair.
My feet are turning hoof.
And Father, see my face
— Skin that was damp and fair
Is barklike and, feel, rough.

See Greytop how I shine.
I rear, break loose, I neigh
Snuffing the air, and harden
Toward a completion, mine.
And next I make my way
Adventuring through your garden.

My play is earnest now.
I canter to and fro.
My blood, it is like light.
Behind an almond bough,
Horns gaudy with its snow,
I wait live, out of sight.

All planned before my birth
For you, Old Man, no other,
Whom your groin's trembling warns.
I stamp upon the earth
A message to my mother.
And then I lower my horns.

Moly

Nightmare of beasthood, snorting, how to wake.
I woke. What beasthood skin she made me take?

Leathery toad that ruts for days on end,
Or cringing dribbling dog, man's servile friend,

Or cat that prettily pounces on its meat,
Tortures it hours, then does not care to eat:

Parrot, moth, shark, wolf, crocodile, ass, flea.
What germs, what jostling mobs there were in me.

These seem like bristles, and the hide is tough.
No claw or web here: each foot ends in hoof.

Into what bulk has method disappeared?
Like ham, streaked. I am gross – grey, gross, flap-eared.

The pale-lashed eyes my only human feature.
My teeth tear, tear. I am the snouted creature

That bites through anything, root, wire, or can.
If I was not afraid I'd eat a man.

Oh a man's flesh already is in mine.
Hand and foot poised for risk. Buried in swine.

I root and root, you think that it is greed,
It is, but I seek out a plant I need.

Direct me gods, whose changes are all holy,
To where it flickers deep in grass, the moly:

Cool flesh of magic in each leaf and shoot,
From milky flower to the black forked root.

From this fat dungeon I could rise to skin
And human title, putting pig within.

I push my big grey wet snout through the green,
Dreaming the flower I have never seen.

For Signs

1

In front of me, the palings of a fence
Throw shadows hard as board across the weeds;
The cracked enamel of a chicken bowl
Gleams like another moon; each clump of reeds
Is split with darkness and yet bristles whole.
The field survives, but with a difference.

2

And sleep like moonlight drifts and clings to shape.
My mind, which learns its freedom every day,
Sinks into vacancy but cannot rest.
While moonlight floods the pillow where it lay,
It walks among the past, weeping, obsessed,
Trying to master it and learn escape.

I dream: the real is shattered and combined,
Until the moon comes back into that sign
It stood in at my birth-hour; and I pass
Back to the field where, statued in the shine,
Someone is gazing upward from the grass
As if toward vaults that honeycomb the mind.

Slight figure in a wide black hat, whose hair
Massed and moon-coloured almost hides his face.
The thin white lips are dry, the eyes intense
Watching not thing, but lunar orgy, chase,
Trap, and cool fantasy of violence.
I recognize the pale long inward stare.

His tight young flesh is only on the top.
Beneath it, is an answering moon, at full,
Pitted with craters and with empty seas.
Dream mentor, I have been inside that skull,
I too have used those cindered passages.

But now the moon leaves Scorpio: I look up.

3

No, not inconstant, though it is called so.
For I have always found it waiting there,
Whether reduced to an invisible seed,
Or whether swollen again above the air
To rake the oubliettes of pain and greed
Opened at night in fellowship below.

It goes, and in its going it returns,
Cycle that I in part am governed by
And cannot understand where it is dark.
I lean upon the fence and watch the sky,
How light fills blinded socket and chafed mark.
It soars, hard, full, and edged, it coldly burns.

Justin

Waiting for her in some small park,
The lamplight's little world clasped round
By sweet rot and the autumn dark,
Once Justin found, or thought he found,
His live flesh flake like onion-skin
From finger-bones where it had held,
And saw the muscle fray within,
Peeling from joints that bunched and swelled.
    The waits had totalled in the shade,
And he had, unaware of debt
Or of expense, already paid
The cost of what he didn't get.
Might she be there? He could not see.
But waiting wears as hard as action,
And he perceived what he would be,
Transparent with dissatisfaction.

Phaedra in the Farm House

From sleep, before first light,
I hear slow-rolling churns
Clank over flags below.
Aches me. The room returns.
I hurt, I wake, I know
The cold dead end of night.

Here father. And here son.
What trust I live between.
But warmth here on the sheet
Is kin-warmth, slow and clean.
I cook the food two eat,
But oh, I sleep with one.

And you, in from the stable.
You spent last evening
Lost in the chalky blues
Of warm hills, rabbitting.
You frown and spell the news,
With forearms on the table.

Tonight, though, we play cards.
You are not playing well.
I smell the oil-lamp's jet,
The parlour's polished smell,
Then you – soap, ghost of sweat,
Tractor oil, and the yards.

Shirt-sleeved you concentrate.
Your moleskin waistcoat glints
Your quick grin never speaks:
I study you for hints
– Hints from those scrubbed boy-cheeks?

I deal a grown man's fate.

The churns wait on in mud:
Tomorrow's milk will sour.
I leave, but bit by bit,
Sharp through the last whole hour.
The chimney will be split,
And that waistcoat be blood.

The Sand Man

Tourists in summer, looking at the view,
    The Bay, the Gate, the Bridge,
From sands that, yearly, city trucks renew,
    Descry him at the postcard's edge.

A white-haired man who hauls up lengths of wood
    And lies beside his fire
Motionless on his side, or gumming food,
    Without a thought, or much desire.

After the beating, thirty-five years since,
    A damaged consciousness
Reduced itself to that mere innocence
    Many have tried to repossess.

Bare to the trunks, the body on the ground
    Is sun-stained, ribbed, and lean:
And slowly in the sand rolls round and round
    In patient reperformed routine.

Sand, sticking to him, keeps him from the dust,
    And armours him about.
Now covered, he has entered that old trust,
    Like sandflies when the tide is out.

He rocks, a blur on ridges, pleased to be.
    Dispersing with the sands
He feels a dry cool multiplicity
    Gilding his body, feet and hands.

Apartment Cats

The Girls wake, stretch, and pad up to the door.
    They rub my leg and purr:
    One sniffs around my shoe,
    Rich with an outside smell,
  The other rolls back on the floor –
White bib exposed, and stomach of soft fur.

Now, more awake, they re-enact Ben Hur
    Along the corridor,
    Wheel, gallop; as they do,
    Their noses twitching still,
  Their eyes get wild, their bodies tense,
Their usual prudence seemingly withdraws.

And then they wrestle: parry, lock of paws,
    Blind hug of close defence,
    Tail-thump, and smothered mew.
    If either, though, feels claws,
  She abruptly rises, knowing well
How to stalk off in wise indifference.

Three

All three are bare.
The father towels himself by two grey boulders
  Long body, then long hair,
Matted like rainy bracken, to his shoulders.

  The pull and risk
Of the Pacific's touch is yet with him:
  He kicked and felt it brisk,
Its cold live sinews tugging at each limb.

  It haunts him still:
Drying his loins, he grins to notice how,
  Struck helpless with the chill,
His cock hangs tiny and withdrawn there now.

  Near, eyes half-closed,
The mother lies back on the hot round stones,
  Her weight to theirs opposed
And pressing them as if they were earth's bones.

  Hard bone, firm skin,
She holds her breasts and belly up, now dry,
  Striped white where clothes have been,
To the heat that sponsors all heat, from the sky.

  Only their son
Is brown all over. Rapt in endless play,
  In which all games make one,
His three-year nakedness is everyday.

Swims as dogs swim.
Rushes his father, wriggles from his hold.
   His body which is him,
Sturdy and volatile, runs off the cold.

      Runs up to me:
Hi there hi there, he shrills, yet will not stop,
   For though continually
Accepting everything his play turns up

      He still leaves it
And comes back to that pebble-warmed recess
   In which the parents sit,
At watch, who had to learn their nakedness.

Words

The shadow of a pine-branch quivered
On a sunlit bank of pale unflowering weed.
  I watched, more solid by the pine,
The dark exactitude that light delivered,
    And, from obsession, or from greed,
      Laboured to make it mine.

  In looking for the words, I found
Bright tendrils, round which that sharp outline faltered:
  Limber detail, no bloom disclosed.
I was still separate on the shadow's ground
    But, charged with growth, was being altered,
      Composing uncomposed.

From the Wave

It mounts at sea, a concave wall
    Down-ribbed with shine,
And pushes forward, building tall
    Its steep incline.

Then from their hiding rise to sight
    Black shapes on boards
Bearing before the fringe of white
    It mottles towards.

Their pale feet curl, they poise their weight
    With a learn'd skill.
It is the wave they imitate
    Keeps them so still.

The marbling bodies have become
    Half wave, half men,
Grafted it seems by feet of foam
    Some seconds, then,

Late as they can, they slice the face
    In timed procession:
Balance is triumph in this place,
    Triumph possession.

The mindless heave of which they rode
    A fluid shelf
Breaks as they leave it, falls and, slowed,
    Loses itself.

Clear, the sheathed bodies slick as seals
    Loosen and tingle;
And by the board the bare foot feels
    The suck of shingle.

They paddle in the shallows still;
    Two splash each other;
Then all swim out to wait until
    The right waves gather.

Tom-Dobbin

centaur poems

1

light is in the pupil
                    luminous seed
and light is in the mind
                       crossing
in an instant
                passage between the two
seamless
            imperceptible transition
skin melting downward into hide
at the centaur's waist
                    there is the one
and at once it is also the other

fair freckled skin, the blond down on it
being at all points
               a beginning
to the glossy chestnut brown which
is also at all points
               a beginning upward

2

Hot in his mind, Tom watches Dobbin fuck,
Watches, and smiles with pleasure, oh what luck.
He sees beyond, and knows he sees, red cows,
Harsh green of grass, and pink-fired chestnut boughs.
The great brown body rears above the mare,
Plunging beneath Tom's interested stare.

In coming Tom and Dobbin join to one –
Only a moment, just as it is done:
A shock of whiteness, shooting like a star,
In which all colours of the spectrum are.

3

He grins, he plunges into orgy. It moves about
him in easy eddies, and he enters their mingling
and branching. He spreads with them, he is veined
with sunshine.

The cobalt gleam of a peacock's neck, the course
of a wind through grasses, distant smoke frozen in
the sky, are extensions of self.

And later something in him rises, neither sun nor
moon, close and brilliant. It lights the debris, and
brings it all together. It grins too, with its own
concentrating passion. It discovers dark shining
tables of rock that rise, inch by inch, out of the
turning waters.

4

The mammal is with her young. She is unique.
Millions of years ago mixed habits gave
That crisp perfected outline, webs, fur, beak.

Risen from her close tunnel to her cave
The duck-billed platypus lies in ripeness till
The line of her belly breaks into a dew.
The brown fur oozes milk for the young one. He,
Hatched into separation, beaks his fill.
If you could see through darkness you could see
One breaking outline that includes the two.

5

Ruthlessly gentle, gently ruthless we move
As if through water with delaying limb.
We circle clasping round an unmarked centre
Gradually closing in, until we enter
The haze together – which is me, which him?
Selves floating in the one flesh we are of.

The Rooftop

White houses bank the hill,
Facing me where I sit.
It should be adequate
To watch the gardens fill

With sunlight, washing tree,
Bush, and the year's last flowers,
And to sit here for hours,
Becoming what I see.

Perception gave me this:
A whole world, bit by bit.
Yet I can not grasp it –
Bits, not an edifice.

Long webs float on the air.
Glistening, they fall and lift.
I turn it down, the gift:
Such fragile lights can tear.

The heat frets earth already,
Harrowed by furious root;
The wireworm takes his loot;
The midday sun is steady.

Petals turn brown and splay:
Loose in a central shell
Seeds whitening dry and swell
Which light fills from decay.

Ruthless in clean unknowing
The plant obeys its need,
And works alone. The seed
Bursts, bare as bone in going,

Bouncing from rot toward earth,
Compound of rot, to wait,
An armoured concentrate
Containing its own birth.

An unseen edifice.
The seen, the tangles, lead
From seed to death to seed
Through green closed passages.

The light drains from the hill.
The gardens rustle, cold,
Huddled in dark, and hold,
Waiting for when they fill.

The Colour Machine

for Mike Caffee

1

Suddenly it is late night, there are people in the basement,
we all sit and lie in front of the colour machine. Someone
among us, at the controls, switches to green and red. Now
the shape in it is riding through a dark red-green sea, it is
like matter approaching and retreating from the brink of
form. Where it has thickened it starts to turn transparent;
where it is almost transparent it starts to thicken. We
cannot tell what it reminds us of: it is in a state of unending
alteration: we can name it only afterwards.

2

Giving himself completely to the colour machine, one of
us became invisible. Being a thing, it does not need gifts,
and anyway what wants something that becomes invisible
as soon as given? It let him go, and he drifted from the
room into a world where he could no longer make an
impression: plants grew into the bridge of his foot, cars
drove through him, he entered movies for free. And of
course, we never saw him again.

I too am a lover, but I am cowardly, selfish, and
calculating. When I most long to give myself, heart, body,
and mind, to the colour machine, I remember our friend,
give a mocking smile, and start making love to curtains. By
means of such promiscuity I can keep myself intact. But I
am uneasy, and hanker for courage and impulsiveness.
Perhaps, for our vanished friend, the moment of giving
made the fact of his disintegration something of negligible

[205]

importance. Or perhaps his consciousness still lives in the intensity of that moment. I am visible and do not know.

1965

Street Song

I am too young to grow a beard
But yes man it was me you heard
In dirty denim and dark glasses.
I look through everyone who passes
But ask him clear, I do not plead,
Keys lids acid and speed.

My grass is not oregano.
Some of it grew in Mexico.
You cannot guess the weed I hold,
Clara Green, Acapulco Gold,
Panama Red, you name it man,
Best on the street since I began.

My methedrine, my double-sun,
Will give you two lives in your one,
Five days of power before you crash.
At which time use these lumps of hash
– They burn so sweet, they smoke so smooth,
They make you sharper while they soothe.

Now here, the best I've got to show,
Made by a righteous cat I know.
Pure acid – it will scrape your brain,
And make it something else again.
Call it heaven, call it hell,
Join me and see the world I sell.

Join me, and I will take you there,
Your head will cut out from your hair
Into whichever self you choose.
With Midday Mick man you can't lose,
I'll get you anything you need.
Keys lids acid and speed.

The Fair in the Woods

to Jere Fransway

The woodsmen blow their horns, and close the day,
Grouped by some logs. The buckskins they are in
Merge with ground's russet and with tree-trunk's grey,
And through the colour of the body's skin
Shift borrowings out of nearby birch and clay.

All day a mounted angel came and went
Sturdily pacing through the trees and crowd,
His brown horse glossy and obedient.
Points glowed among his hair: dark-haired, dark-browed.
He supervised a god's experiment.

Some clustered in the upper boughs, from where
They watched the groups beneath them make their way,
Children of light, all different, through the fair,
Pulsing among the pulsing trunks. And they,
The danglers, ripened in the brilliant air.

Upon a platform dappled by the sun
The whole speed-family in a half round clapped
About the dancer where she arched and spun.
They raced toward stillness till they overlapped,
Ten energies working inward through the one.

Landscape of acid:
                    where on fern and mound
The lights fragmented by the roofing bough
Throbbed outward, joining over broken ground
To one long dazzling burst; as even now
Horn closes over horn into one sound.

Knuckle takes back its colour, nail its line.
Slowly the tawny jerkins separate
From bark and earth, but they will recombine
In the autumnal dusk, for it is late.
The horns call. There is little left to shine.

LSD, San Rafael Woods: 'Renaissance Fair'

Listening to Jefferson Airplane

in the Polo Grounds, Golden Gate Park

The music comes and goes on the wind,
Comes and goes on the brain.

To Natty Bumppo

The grey eyes watchful and a lightened hand.
The ruder territory opening up
Fills with discovery: unoutlined land
With which familiar places overlap.

A feeling forward, or a being aware.
I reach, out, on: beyond the elm-topped rise
There is, not yet but forming now, a there
To be completed by the opened eyes.

A plain, a forest, a field full of folk.
Footing the sun-shot turf beneath the trees,
They brandish their arms upward like the oak,
Their sky-blue banners rest along the breeze.

Open on all sides, it is held in common,
The first field of a glistening continent
Each found by trusting Eden in the human:
The guiding hand, the bright grey eyes intent.

The Garden of the Gods

All plants grow here; the most minute,
   Glowing from turf, is in its place.
   The constant vision of the race:
Lawned orchard deep with flower and fruit.

So bright, that some who see it near,
   Think there is lapis on the stems,
   And think green, blue, and crimson gems
Hang from the vines and briars here.

They follow path to path in wonder
   Through the intense undazzling light.
   Nowhere does blossom flare so white!
Nowhere so black is earthmould under!

It goes, though it may come again.
   But if at last they try to tell,
   They search for trope or parallel,
And cannot, after all, explain.

It was sufficient, there, to be,
   And meaning, thus, was superseded.
   – Night circles it, it has receded,
Distant and difficult to see.

Where my foot rests, I hear the creak
   From generations of my kin,
   Layer on layer, pressed leaf-thin.
They merely are. They cannot speak.

This was the garden's place of birth:
    I trace it downward from my mind,
    Through breast and calf I feel it vined,
And rooted in the death-rich earth.

Flooded Meadows

In sunlight now, after the weeks it rained,
Water has mapped irregular shapes that follow
Between no banks, impassive where it drained
Then stayed to rise and brim from every hollow.
Hillocks are firm, though soft, and not yet mud.
Tangles of long bright grass, like waterweed,
Surface upon the patches of the flood,
Distinct as islands from their valleys freed
And sharp as reefs dividing inland seas.
Yet definition is suspended, for,
In pools across the level listlessness,
Light answers only light before the breeze,
Cancelling the rutted, weedy, slow brown floor
For the unity of unabsorbed excess.

Grasses

Laurel and eucalyptus, dry sharp smells,
Pause in the dust of summer. But we sit
High on a fort, above grey blocks and wells,
And watch the restless grasses lapping it.

Each dulling-green, keen, streaky blade of grass
Leans to one body when the breezes start:
A one-time pathway flickers as they pass,
Where paler toward the root the quick ranks part.

The grasses quiver, rising from below.
I wait on warm rough concrete, I have time.
They round off all the lower steps, and blow
Like lights on bended water as they climb.

From some dark passage in the abandoned fort,
I hear a friend's harmonica – withdrawn sound,
A long whine drawling after several short . . .
The spiky body mounting from the ground.

A wail uneven all the afternoon,
Thin, slow, no noise of tramping nor of dance.
It is the sound, half tuneless and half tune,
With which the scattered details make advance.

Kirby's Cove

The Messenger

Is this man turning angel as he stares
At one red flower whose name he does not know,
   The velvet face, the black-tipped hairs?

His eyes dilated like a cat's at night,
His lips move somewhat but he does not speak
   Of what completes him through his sight.

His body makes to imitate the flower,
Kneeling, with splayed toes pushing at the soil,
   The source, crude, granular, and sour.

His stillness answers like a looking glass
The flower's, it is repose of unblown flame
   That nests within the glow of grass.

Later the news, to branch from sense and sense,
Bringing their versions of the flower in small
   Outward into intelligence.

But meanwhile, quiet and reaching as a flame,
He bends, gazing not at but into it,
   Tough stalk, and face without a name.

Being Born

The tanker slips behind a distant ridge
And, on the blue, a formal S of smoke
Still hangs. I send myself out on my look.
But just beyond my vision, at the edge

To left and right, there reach or seem to reach
Margins, vague pillars, not quite visible,
Or unfleshed giant presences so tall
They stretch from top to bottom, sky to beach.

What memory loosed, of man and boundary blended?
One tug, one more, and I could have it here.
– Yes that's it, ah two shapes begin to clear:
Midwife and doctor faintly apprehended.

I let them both almost solidify,
Their quiet activity bit by bit outlined,
Clean hand and calm eye, but still view behind,
Bright crinkling foam, headland, and level sky.

I think of being grabbed from the warm sand,
Shiny red bawling newborn with clenched eyes,
Slapped into life; and as it clarifies
My friends recede, alas the dwindling land.

Must I rewrite my childhood? What jagg'd growth
What mergings of authority and pain,
Invading breath, must I live through again?
Are they the past or yet to come or both?

Both. Between moving air and moving ocean
The tanker pushes, squat and purposeful,
But elsewhere. And the smoke. Though now air's pull
Begins to suck it into its own motion.

There is a furnace that connects them there.
The metal, guided, cuts through fall and lift,
While the coils from it widen, spread, and drift
To feed the open currents of the air.

At the Centre

What place is this

                       Cracked wood steps led me here.
The gravelled roof is fenced in where I stand.
But it is open, I am not confined
By weathered boards or barbed wire at the stair,
From which rust crumbles black-red on my hand.
If it is mine. It looks too dark and lined.

What sky

              A pearly damp grey covers it
Almost infringing on the lighted sign
Above Hamm's Brewery, a huge blond glass
Filling as its component lights are lit.
You cannot keep them. Blinking line by line
They brim beyond the scaffold they replace.

2

What is this steady pouring that

                       Oh, wonder.
The blue line bleeds and on the gold one draws.
Currents of image widen, braid, and blend
– Pouring in cascade over me and under –
To one all-river. Fleet it does not pause,
The sinewy flux pours without start or end.

What place is this
                And what is it that broods
Barely beyond its own creation's course,
And not abstracted from it, not the Word,
But overlapping like the wet low clouds
The rivering images – their unstopped source,
Its roar unheard from being always heard.

What am
            Though in the river, I abstract
Fence, word, and notion. On the stream at full
A flurry, where the mind rides separate!
But this brief cresting, sharpened and exact,
Is fluid too, is open to the pull
And on the underside twined deep with it.

3

Terror and beauty in a single board.
The rough grain in relief – a tracery
Fronded and ferned, of woods inside the wood.
Splinter and scar – I saw them too, they poured.
White paint-chip and the overhanging sky:
The flow-lines faintly traced or understood.

Later, downstairs and at the kitchen table,
I look round at my friends. Through light we move
Like foam. We started choosing long ago
– Clearly and capably as we were able –
Hostages from the pouring we are of.
The faces are as bright now as fresh snow.

LSD, Folsom Street

[221]

The Discovery of the Pacific

They lean against the cooling car, backs pressed
Upon the dust of a brown continent,
And watch the sun, now Westward of their West,
Fall to the ocean. Where it led they went.

Kansas to California. Day by day
They travelled emptier of the things they knew.
They improvised new habits on the way,
But lost the occasions, and then lost them too.

One night, no one and nowhere, she had woken
To resin-smell and to the firs' slight sound,
And through their sleeping-bag had felt the broken
Tight-knotted surfaces of the naked ground.

Only his lean quiet body cupping hers
Kept her from it, the extreme chill. By degrees
She fell asleep. Around them in the firs
The wind probed, tiding through forked estuaries.

And now their skin is caked with road, the grime
Merely reflecting sunlight as it fails.
They leave their clothes among the rocks they climb,
Blunt leaves of iceplant nuzzle at their soles.

Now they stand chin-deep in the sway of ocean,
Firm West, two stringy bodies face to face,
And come, together, in the water's motion,
The full caught pause of their embrace.

Sunlight

Some things, by their affinity light's token,
Are more than shown: steel glitters from a track;
Small glinting scoops, after a wave has broken,
Dimple the water in its draining back;

Water, glass, metal, match light in their raptures,
Flashing their many answers to the one.
What captures light belongs to what it captures:
The whole side of a world facing the sun,

Re-turned to woo the original perfection,
Giving itself to what created it,
And wearing green in sign of its subjection.
It is as if the sun were infinite.

But angry flaws are swallowed by the distance;
It varies, moves, its concentrated fires
Are slowly dying – the image of persistence
Is an image, only, of our own desires:

Desires and knowledge touch without relating.
The system of which sun and we are part
Is both imperfect and deteriorating.
And yet the sun outlasts us at the heart.

Great seedbed, yellow centre of the flower,
Flower on its own, without a root or stem,
Giving all colour and all shape their power,
Still recreating in defining them,

Enable us, altering like you, to enter
Your passionless love, impartial but intense,
And kindle in acceptance round your centre,
Petals of light lost in your innocence.

Jack Straw's Castle (1976)

I

The Bed

The pulsing stops where time has been,
    The garden is snow-bound,
The branches weighed down and the paths filled in,
    Drifts quilt the ground.

We lie soft-caught, still now it's done,
    Loose-twined across the bed
Like wrestling statues; but it still goes on
    Inside my head.

Diagrams

Downtown, an office tower is going up.
And from the mesa of unfinished top
Big cranes jut, spectral points of stiffened net:
Angled top-heavy artefacts, and yet
Diagrams from the sky, as if its air
Could drop lines, snip them off, and leave them there.

On girders round them, Indians pad like cats,
With wrenches in their pockets and hard hats.

They wear their yellow boots like moccasins,
Balanced where air ends and where steel begins,
Sky men, and through the sole's flesh, chewed and pliant,
They feel the studded bone-edge of the giant.
It grunts and sways through its whole metal length.
And giving to the air is sign of strength.

Iron Landscapes
                    (and the Statue of Liberty)

No trellises, no vines
                    a fire escape
Repeats a bare black Z from tier to tier.
Hard flower, tin scroll embellish this landscape.
Between iron columns I walk toward the pier.

And stand a long time at the end of it
Gazing at iron on the New Jersey side.
A girdered ferry-building opposite,
Displaying the name LACKAWANNA, seems to ride

The turbulent brown-grey waters that intervene:
Cool seething incompletion that I love.
The zigzags come and go, sheen tracking sheen;
And water wrestles with the air above.

But I'm at peace with the iron landscape too,
Hard because buildings must be hard to last
– Block, cylinder, cube, built with their angles true,
A dream of righteous permanence, from the past.

In Nixon's era, decades after the ferry,
The copper embodiment of the pieties
Seems hard, but hard like a revolutionary
With indignation, constant as she is.

From here you can glimpse her downstream, her far charm,
Liberty, tiny woman in the mist
– You cannot see the torch – raising her arm
Lorn, bold, as if saluting with her fist.

Morton Street Pier, New York, May 1973

The Corporal

Half of my youth I watched the soldiers
And saw mechanic clerk and cook
Subsumed beneath a uniform.
Grey black and khaki was their look
Whose tool and instrument was death.

I watched them wheel on white parade grounds.
How could the flesh have such control?
Ballets with symmetry of the flower
Outlined the aspect of a soul
Whose pure precision was of death.

I saw them radiate from the barracks
Into the town that it was in.
Girl-hungry loutish casanovas,
Their wool and webbing grated skin
For small forgettings as in death.

One I remember best, a corporal
I'd notice clumping to and fro
Piratical along my street,
When I was about fifteen or so
And my passion and concern was death.

Caught by the bulk's fine inward flicker,
The white-toothed smile he turned to all,
Who would not have considered him
Unsoldierly as an animal,
Being the bright reverse of death?

Yet something fixed outlined the impulse.
His very health was dressed to kill.
He had the acrobat's love of self
– Balancing body was his skill
Against the uniform space of death.

Fever

Impatient all the foggy day for night
   You plunged into the bar eager to loot.
A self-defeating eagerness: you're light,
   You change direction and shift from foot to foot,
Too skittish to be capable of repose
   Or of deciding what is worth pursuit.

Your mother thought you beautiful, I suppose,
   She dandled you all day and watched your sleep.
Perhaps that's half the trouble. And it grows:
   An unattended conqueror now, you keep
Getting less beautiful toward the evening's end.
   The boy's potential sours to malice, deep
Most against those who've done nothing to offend.
   They did not notice you, and only I
Have watched you much – though not as covert friend
   But picturing roles reversed, with you the spy.

The lights go up. What glittering audience
   Tier above tier notices finally
Your ragged defeat, your jovial pretence?
   You stand still, but the bar is emptying fast.
Time to go home babe, though now you feel most tense.
   These games have little content. If you've lost
It doesn't matter tomorrow. Sleep well. Heaven knows
   Feverish people need more sleep than most
And need to learn all they can about repose.

The Night Piece

The fog drifts slowly down the hill
And as I mount gets thicker still,
Closes me in, makes me its own
Like bedclothes on the paving stone.

Here are the last few streets to climb,
Galleries, run through veins of time,
Almost familiar, where I creep
Toward sleep like fog, through fog like sleep.

Last Days at Teddington

The windows wide through day and night
Gave on the garden like a room.
The garden smell, green composite,
Flowed in and out a house in bloom.

To the shaggy dog who skidded from
The concrete through the kitchen door
To yellow-squared linoleum,
It was an undivided floor.

How green it was indoors. The thin
Pale creepers climbed up brick until
We saw their rolled tongues flicker in
Across the cracked paint of the sill.

How sociable the garden was.
We ate and talked in given light.
The children put their toys to grass
All the warm wakeful August night.

So coming back from drinking late
We picked our way below the wall
But in the higher grass, dewed wet,
Stumbled on tricycle and ball.

When everything was moved away,
The house returned to board and shelf,
And smelt of hot dust through the day,
The garden fell back on itself.

All Night, Legs Pointed East

All night, legs pointed east, I shift around
Inside myself, to breast to crotch to head.
Or freed from catnaps to the teeming night
I float, and pinpoint the minutest sound.
I don't know why I doze my time in bed.

An air moves in, I catch the damp plain smells.
But outside, after winter's weeks of rain
The soil of gardens breaks and dries a bit:
A trough between two San Francisco hills
Where granules hold warmth round them as they drain.

Tonight reminds me of my teens in spring –
Not sexual really, it's a plant's unrest
Or bird's expectancy, that enters full
On its conditions, quick eye claw and wing
Submitting to its pulse, alert in the nest.

Toward the night's end the body lies back, still,
Caught in mid-turn by sleep however brief.
In stealth I fill and fill it out. At dawn
Like loosened soil that packs a grassy hill
I fill it wholly, here, hungry for leaf.

The Geysers

They are in Sonoma County, California. You could camp anywhere you wanted in the area for a dollar a day, but it was closed down in 1973. There was also a bath house, containing hot and cool pools. It was about seventy years old: it may have originally been open to the sky, but in the seventies it was roughly covered in with sections of green corrugated plastic.

Thou hast thy walkes for health, as well as sport.

I *Sleep by the Hot Stream*

Gentle as breathing
                    down to us it spills
From geysers heard but hidden in the hills.
Those starlit scalps are parched blond; where we lie,
The small flat patch of earth fed evenly
By warmth and wet, there's dark grass fine as hair.

This is our bedroom, where we learn the air,
Our sleeping bags laid out in the valley's crotch.
I lie an arm-length from the stream and watch
Arcs fading between stars. There
                                    bright! faint! gone!
More meteors than I've ever set eyes on:
The flash-head vanishing as it is defined,
Its own end streaking like a wake behind.

I must have been asleep when morning came.
The v-sides of our shadowed valley frame
The tall hill fair with sunshine opposite.
Live-oaks are of it yet crest separate,

In heavy festooned arches. Now it's day
We get up naked as we intend to stay.

Gentle as breathing
                Sleep by the hot stream, broken.
Bright, faint, and gone. What I am now has woken.

2   *The Cool Stream*

People are wading up the stream all day,
People are swimming, people are at play.

Two birds like one dart upstream toward the falls,
A keen brown thrust between the canyon walls.

Those walls are crammed with neighbouring detail,
Small as an ocean rock-pool's, and no more frail:
Pigmy fern groves, a long web slung across
A perilous bush, an emerald fur of moss;
Wherever it is possible, some plant
Growing in crevices or up a slant.

Sun at meridian shines between the walls
And here below, the talking animals
Enter an unclaimed space, like plants and birds,
And fill it out without too many words
Treating of other places they have been.
I see a little snake alert in its skin
Striped head and neck from water, unmoving, reared:
Tongue-flicker, and a fly has disappeared.
What elegance! it does not watch itself.

Above, wet rounded limbs stretched on a shelf,
The rock glimpsed through blond drying wisps of hair.

A little beach and, barking at the air
Then pacing, pacing, a marooned brown dog.

And some are trying to straddle a floating log,
Some rest and pass a joint, some climb the fall:
Tan black and pink, firm shining bodies, all
Move with a special unconsidered grace.
For though we have invaded this glittering place
And broke the silences, yet we submit:
So wholly, that we are details of it.

3 *The Geyser*
Heat from the sky, and from the rubble of stones.

The higher the more close-picked are Earth's bones:
A climb through moonland, tortured pocked and grey.
Beside the steep path where I make my way
Small puffs of steam bloom out at intervals,
And hot deposit seeps from soggy holes
Scabbing to yellow or wet reddish brown.

I reach the top: the geyser on the crown
Which from the distance was a smart panache
Is merely a searing column of steam from ash.

A cinderfield that lacks all skin of soil,
It has no complication, no detail,
The force too simple and big to comprehend,
Like a beginning, also like an end.
No customs I have learned can make me wise
To deal with such. And I do recognize
– For what such recognition may be worth –
Fire at my centre, burning since my birth

Under the pleasant flesh. Force calls to force.
Up here a man might shrivel in his source.

4   *The Bath House*
Night
        heat
                the hot bath, barely endurable.
Closer than that rank sulphurous smell
a sharp-sweet drifting fume of dope.
Down from half-lucent roofing   moonrays slope
(by the plastic filtered green)
                                to candleflicker below.
Water brims at my chin
                        breath coming slow
All round me faces bob   old men, pubescent girls
sweat rolls down foreheads from wet curls
bodies locked soft in trance of heat   not saying much
eyes empty
                Other senses breaking down to touch
touch of skin   of hot water on the skin
I grasp my mind
                squeeze open
                            touch within

And grope
        it is hazy suddenly
                            it is strange
        labouring through uneasy change
whether toward ecstasy or panic
                                wish I knew

no longer know for certain who is who
Am I supposed to recognize
those bearded boys   or her, with dreaming eyes

. . . . . .

Not certain
      who I am or where
weight of a darker earlier air

the body heavily buoyant
           sheathed by heat
hard, almost, with it
          Upward, from my feet
I feel rise in me a new kind of blood
The water round me thickens to hot mud
Sunk in it
      passive   plated   slow
stretching my coils on coils
          And still I grow
and barely move in years I am so great

I exist I hardly can be said to wait

Till waking one night I look up to see
new gods are shining over me
    What flung Orion's belt across the sky?
I lived the age of reptiles out
          and I

. . . . . .

lighten, diminish
                    in the dream, halfdream
halfdream, reality
                    of flickering stream

beneath mud
            branching
                        branching streams run through
through me
            the mud breathes
                        breathes me too

and bobbing in the womb, all round me Mother
I am part of all   there is no other
I extend into
            her mind   her mountainous knees
red meadows   salty seas
birdbone and pulp, unnamed, unborn
                                    I live

                    . .   . .   . .

It tore
      what flash cut
                    made me fugitive
caesarian lightning lopped me off separate

and born in flight from the world
                                    but through it, into it
aware now (piercingly)
                    of my translation
each sense raw-healed   in sudden limitation

I hurry, what I did I do not know
nor who pursues, nor why I go
I crawl along moon-dappled tunnels
                                    climb
look back:
            they marked me all the time
shadows that lengthen over whitened fields below
calm, closing in
                  Not all the plants that grow
thickets of freckled foxglove, rank hedgerow,
bowed bushes, laurel, woods of oak could hide me
But now
            I see the stream that bends beside me

quiet and deep, a refuge I could stay within
reminding me of somewhere I have been

hearing their tread
                  I dive in
                              sink beneath
wait hid in
            cool security
                        I cannot breathe
I burst for oxygen
shoot upward, then
break through
                  another surface
                              where I meet

                  . .   . .   . .

dreamers
            the faces bobbing round me on the heat
green moonlight, smell of dope

                 the shining arms   and eyes
staring at me without surprise
I am trapped
        It will begin
pubescent girl and bearded boy close in

I give up
       hope   as they move in on me

loosened so quickly from it   I am free

I brace myself light strong and clear
and understand why I came here

entering their purpose as they enter mine

I am part of all
        hands take
             hands tear and twine

I yielded
     oh, the yield
          what have I slept?
my blood is yours   the hands that take accept

          . . . . . .

torn from the self
         in which I breathed and trod
I am

   I am raw meat

      I am a god

Three Songs

Baby Song

From the private ease of Mother's womb
I fall into the lighted room.

Why don't they simply put me back
Where it is warm and wet and black?

But one thing follows on another.
Things were different inside Mother.

Padded and jolly I would ride
The perfect comfort of her inside.

They tuck me in a rustling bed
— I lie there, raging, small, and red.

I may sleep soon, I may forget,
But I won't forget that I regret.

A rain of blood poured round her womb,
But all time roars outside this room.

Hitching into Frisco

Truck put me off on Fell.
I'll walk to Union Square
And watch the homeless there
From jailhouse and hotel.

And liable to none.
I've heard the long freight trains,
The cars marked with home names.
Mom wouldn't know her son.

I was a gentle boy.
That dusty Texas town
Was good for settling down.
The girls were clean and coy.

Had everywhere to go,
And thumbed around the nation.
It's like improvisation
Inside a tune you know.

The highways in the bone
Phrase after phrase unwind.
For all I leave behind
There is a new song grown.

And everywhere to go.

Sparrow
Chill to the marrow
pity poor Sparrow
got any change Sir
Sparrow needs change Sir

I stand here in the cold
in a loose old suit bruised and dirty
I may look fifty years old
but I'm only thirty

My feet smell bad and they ache
the wine's gone sour and stale in my pores
my throat is sand I shake
and I live out of doors

I shelter from the rain
in a leaky doorway in leaky shoes
and all I have is pain
that's left to lose

I need some change for a drink
of sweet wine Sir a bottle of sherry
it's the sugar in it I think
will make me merry

I'll be a daredevil then
millionaire stud in my right mind
a jewel among men
if you'll be so kind

The bastard passed me by
fuck you asshole that's what I say
I hope I see you cry
like Sparrow one day

2

. . . and when he pictured in his mind the ugly chamber, false and quiet, false and quiet through the dark hours of two nights, and the tumbled bed, and he not in it, though believed to be, he became in a manner his own ghost and phantom, and was at once the haunting spirit and the haunted man.

Martin Chuzzlewit

The Plunge

down a rope of
bubbles

trapped where you
chose to come
                    it
is all there is

the brute thrust of
entering this all-
alien like a bitter
sheath
          each
nerve each
atom of skin
tightens against it
to a gliding
a moving with —
if flesh could
become water it

unlost
          plying
a blurred sunken sky where
you carry your own
pale home with you

at rest in your own
prolonged ache

and the testing forward
how much more can the body
take, how much dare
it is all there is

till
the body
knows now it's
time, lets go ah
holding
almost till too late
gives itself to the slow
rejection
you go limp on it, a
gentle lift, you
wait on it, wait
you

eat the air

Bringing to Light

powder, chunks of road, twisted
skeletal metal, clay
               I think
of ancient cities of bringing to light
foundations under the foundations

bringing a raft of tiny
cellars to light of day:
gold pocks in the
broad sunlight, craters
like a honeycomb bared

. . . . . .

In one cellar, a certain mannekin
terribly confined
in his sweat and beard
went crazy as Bothwell.
In another, his jailer lived,
here are his shelves for
cup and smock. He was a jailer
so knew he was free.

. . . . . .

Every day the luminous tiers
of the city are filmed with a dust,
a light silt from foot and flesh
and the travelling mind.

. . . . . .

I have forgotten a picnic on a hill
in Kent when I was six, but
have a page of snapshots about it.
It still takes place, but in
a cellar I cannot locate.

There is a cellar, a cell, a cellular
room where a handsome spirit
of wilfulness picnics with me
all day limber imaginary brother
dandling me between his feet
kissing my eyes and mouth
and genitals making me
all his own all day
                    as he is mine.

                . . . . . .

But beneath the superior cellars
others reach downward
                            floor under
floor Babel reversed

Opening doors I discover
the debris of sorcery interrupted
    bone structures like experiments

fewer and fewer
joining each other in their origins

separate words return to their roots
lover and mother melt into
one figure that covers its face
nameless and inescapable

need arrayed like a cause

Achilles and Achelous the rivergod
he fought unite in person
and in name as the earlier
Achelous who precedes both

tress of the Greek's hair red-glinting
braids with thick riverweed
the cell darkens with braiding
toward their common root
in the lowest the last the
first cavern, dark and moist
of which
           the foundations
are merely the Earth

          . .   . . . .

nothing
        but a faint
smell, mushroomy, thin
as if something
                 even here
were separating from its dam

a separating
             of cells

Thomas Bewick

I think of a man on foot
going through thick woods,
a buckle on his brimmed hat,
a stick in his hand.

He comes on from the deep
shadow now to the gladed parts
where light speckles the ground
like scoops out of darkness.

Gnarled branches reaching down
their green gifts; weed reaching up
milky flower and damp leaf.

I think of a man fording
a pebbly stream. A rock
is covered in places with
minute crops of moss
– frail stalks of yellow rising
from the green, each
bloom of it distinct, as
he notices. He notices
the bee's many-jointed legs and its
papery wings veined like leaf,
or the rise of a frog's back
into double peaks, and this morning
by a stile he noticed ferns
afloat on air.

                    Drinking from
clear stream and resting
on the rock he loses himself
in detail,
            he reverts
to an earlier self, not yet
separate from what it sees,

a selfless self as difficult
to recover and hold as to
capture the exact way
a burly bluetit grips
its branch (leaning forward)
over this rock
                    and in
The History of British Birds.

Wrestling

for Robert Duncan

Discourse
          of sun and moon
fire and beginnings

behind words
          the illuminated words

A palimpsest
          the disco urse having been
          erased and replaced with
          words of a role
          but if you hold
          the parchment to light
          you may see
                    the discourse
          where the stylus pressed
          the fat, where it has
          always held, continuing
          luminous behind.
          the covering script
          transparent to it.
          no secret
                    clear,
          still, like a high
          window you never noticed
          it lets in light

continual discourse
         of angels
         and sons of angels
         of semen, of beginnings
lucid accounts of flight
         arms for wings

a tale of wrestling with a stranger
         a stranger, like
         a man, like

a messenger
         loping, compact
         in familiar places
         he moves with that
         separate grace, that
         sureness of foot
         you know in
         animal and angel

messages from
         sun and moon
picked up
         on waves, interpreted

the sun and moon, for
         signs, for seasons
         hang in darkness
         visible mysteries
         fire
         and reflected fire

language of
        tides and seasons
luminous discourse
        telling about
        beginnings

The Outdoor Concert

At the edge
of the understanding:
        it's the secret.

You recognize not
the content of it but
the fact that it is
there to be recognized.

Dust raised
by vendors and dancers
shimmers on the windless air
where it hovers
as if it will never settle.

The secret
is still the secret

is not a proposition:
it's in finding
what connects the man
with the music, with
the listeners, with the fog
in the top of the eucalyptus,
with dust discovered on the lip

and then in living a while
at that luminous intersection,
spread at the centre
like a white garden spider
so still
that you think it
has become its web,

a god existing
only in its creation.

Saturnalia

The time of year comes
round, the campagna
is stone and grey stalk

Once again outlaws
in majority, the throng
bursts from street to
street
      one body
no longer creeping through
a conduit of mossed stone
or marble it is a
muscled flood, still
rising still reshaping

licence awakes us

finding our likeness in
being bare, we
have thrown off
the variegated stuffs that
distinguished us one from
one
     here in orgy
a Laocoön of twined
limbs, in open
incest reaching through to
ourselves in others

beloved flesh

the whole body pulses
like an erection, blood
in the head and furious
with tenderness
                    the senses
mingle, before returning
sharpened to their homes,
they roam at play through
each organ as if
each were
                    equally
a zone of Eros

Faustus Triumphant

The dazzled blood
submits, carries the
flame through me to every
organ till blood itself
is flamy
            flame animates me
with delight in time's things
so intense that I am
almost lost to time

Already vining the
arbours of my body, flame
starts from my fingers!
now my flame-limbs wrap round
marble   ebony   fur   flesh
without combusting what
they embrace. I
lick everything.
                        What
tracks led

            there.
and there and there
where I pricked the
arm where I
got the blood to sign

I remember there was
a bargain made but I
think I'm safe. For
vein and artery are not
store keepers, nor is
Nature a lawyer.

My joy so great
that if hell threatens, the
memory alone of flame
protects me. There is
no terror in combustion.
I shall rejoice to
enter into him
                    Father-
Nature, the Great Flame

Dolly

You recognize it like
the smell of the sour chemical
that gets into the sweat
of some people from
birth onward.

        And you say
he's out to end his choices
for good and doesn't realize it.

I know someone who
was never let play with dolls
when he was little, so now
(he thinks to spite his father)
collects them.
But it's the crippled ones
he cherishes most, particularly
the quadriplegics: they loll
blank stomachs depending from blank heads
with no freedom
                ever, ever

and in need.

Jack Straw's Castle

Jack Straw sits
           sits in his castle
Jack Straw watches the rain

why can't I leave my castle
he says, isn't there anyone
anyone here besides me

sometimes I find myself wondering
if the castle is castle at all
a place apart, or merely
the castle that every snail
must carry around till his death

and then there's the matter of breath
on a cold day it rears before me
like a beautiful fern
I'm amazed at the plant

will it survive me
a man of no account
visited only by visions

and no one here
no one who knows how to play

visions, voices, burning smells
all of a rainy day

2

Pig Pig she cries
I can hear her from next door
He fucked me in the mouth
and now he won't give me car fare
she rages and cries

3

The rain stops. I look round: a square of floor,
Blond wood, shines palely in the laggard sun;
The kittens suck, contrasting strips of fur,
The mother in their box, a perfect fit;
I finally got it how I wanted it,
A fine snug house when all is said and done.

But night makes me uneasy: floor by floor
Rooms never guessed at open from the gloom
First as thin smoky lines, ghost of a door
Or lintel that develops like a print
Darkening into full embodiment
– Boudoir and oubliette, room on room on room.

And I have met or I believed I met
People in some of them, though they were not
The kind I need. They looked convincing, yet
There always was too much of the phantom to them.
Meanwhile, and even when I walked right through them,
I was talking, talking to myself. Of what?

Fact was, the echo of each word drowned out
The next word spoken, and I cannot say
What it was I was going on about.

It could be I was asking, Do these rooms
Spring up at night-time suddenly, like mushrooms,
Or have they all been hiding here all day?

4
Dream sponsors:
Charles Manson, tongue
playing over dry lips,
thinking a long thought;
and the Furies, mad
puppety heads appearing
in the open transom above
a forming door, like heads
of kittens staring angrily
over the edge of their box:

'Quick, fetch Medusa,'
their shrewish voices,
'Show him Medusa.'

Maybe I won't turn away,
maybe I'm so cool
I could outstare her.

5
The door opens.
There are no snakes.
The head
is on the table.

On the table
gold hair struck

by light from
the naked bulb,
a dazzle in which
the ground of dazzle
is consumed, the
hair burning
in its own gold.

And her eyes
gaze at me,
pale blue, but
blank as the eyes
of zombie or angel,
with the stunned
lack of expression
of one
who has beheld
the source of everything
and found it
the same as nothing.

In her dazzle I
catch fire
self-delighting
self-sufficient
self-consuming
till
I burn out
so heavy
I sink into
darkness into
my foundations.

6

Down in the cellars, nothing is visible

                                            no one

Though there's a sound about me of many breathing
Light slap of foot on stone and rustle of body
Against body and stone.

                              And when later

I finger a stickiness along the ridges
Of a large central block that feels like granite
I don't know if it's my own, or I shed it,
Or both, as if priest and victim were only
Two limbs of the same body.

                                The lost traveller.

For this is the seat of needs

                          so deep, so old

That even where eye never perceives body
And where the sharpest ear discerns only
The light slap and rustle of flesh on stone
They, the needs, seek ritual and ceremony
To appease themselves

                        (Oh, the breathing all around me)

Or they would tear apart the life that feeds them.

7

I am the man on the rack.
I am the man who puts the man on the rack.
I am the man who watches the man who puts the man on the
    rack.

8

Might it not have been
a thought-up film
which suddenly ceases

the lights go up
I can see only
this pearl-grey chamber
false and quiet
no audience here
just the throned one

nothing outside the bone
nothing accessible

the ambush and taking of
meaning were nothing
                              were
inventions of Little Ease

I sit
trapped in bone
I am back again
where I never left, I sit
in my first instant, where
I never left

petrified at my centre

9

I spin like a solitary star, I swoon.

But there breaks into my long solitude

A bearded face, it's Charlie, close as close,
His breath that stinks of jail – of pain and fungus,
So close that I breathe nothing else.

Then I recall as if it were my own
Life on the hot ranch, and the other smells.
Of laurel in the sun, fierce, sweet; of people
– Death-sweat or lust-sweat they smelt much the same.
He reigned in sultry power over his dream.

I come back to the face pushed into mine.
Tells me he's bound to point out, man,
That dreams don't come from nowhere: it's your dream
He says, you dreamt it. So there's no escape.

And now he's squatting at a distance
To wait the taunt's effect, paring his nails,
From time to time glancing up sideways at me,
A sly mad look. Yes, but he's not mad either.

He's gone too far, Charlie you've overdone it.
Something inside my head turns over.
I think I see how his taunt can be my staircase,
For if I brought all of this stuff inside
There must be an outside to bring it from.
Outside the castle, somewhere, there must be
A real Charles Manson, a real woman crying,
And laws I had no hand in, like gravity.

About midnight. Where earlier there had seemed
A shadowy arch projected on the bone-like stone,
I notice, fixing itself,
Easing itself in place even as I see it,
A staircase leading upward.
                                        Is that rain
Far overhead, that drumming sound?
Boy, what a climb ahead.

At the bottom, looking back, I find
He is, for now at any rate, clean gone.

10

My coldness wakes me,
mine, and the kitchen chair's.

How long have I sat here? I
went to sleep in bed.

Entering real rooms perhaps,
my own spectre, cold,

unshivering as a flight of
flint steps that leads nowhere,

in a ruin, where the wall
abruptly ends, and the steps too

and you stare down at the broken
slabs far below, at the ivy

glinting over bone-chips which must
at one time have been castle.

11

Down panic, down. The castle is still here,
And I am in the kitchen with a beer
Hearing the hurricane thin out to rain.
Got to relax if I'm to sleep again.
The castle is here, but not snug any more,
I'm loose, I rattle in its hollow core.
And as for that parade of rooms – shed, jail,

[277]

Cellar, each snapping at the next one's tail –
That raced inside my skull for half the night,
I hope I'm through with that. I flick the light.
And though the dungeon will be there for good
(What laid those stones?) at least I found I could,
Thrown down, escape by learning what to learn;
And hold it that held me.
                                    Till I return.

And so to bed, in hopes that I won't dream.

                            . .   . .   . .

I drift, doze, sleep. But toward dawn it does seem,
While I half-wake, too tired to turn my head,
That someone stirs behind me in the bed
Between two windows on an upper floor.
Is it a real man muttering? I'm not sure.
Though he does not seem phantom-like as yet,
Thick, heavily breathing, with a sweet faint sweat.

So humid, we lie sheetless – bare and close,
Facing apart, but leaning ass to ass.
And that mere contact is sufficient touch,
A hinge, it separates but not too much.
An air moves over us, as calm and cool
As the green water of a swimming pool.

What if this is the man I gave my key
Who got in while I slept? Or what if he,
Still, is a dream of that same man?
                                        No, real.
Comes from outside the castle, I can feel.
The beauty's in what is, not what may seem.

I turn. And even if he were a dream
– Thick sweating flesh against which I lie curled –
With dreams like this, Jack's ready for the world.

1973–4

An Amorous Debate

Leather Kid and Fleshly

Birds whistled, all
Nature was doing something while
Leather Kid and Fleshly
lay on a bank and
gleamingly discoursed
                like this:
'You are so strong,' she said, 'such
a firm defence of hide against
the ripple of skin, it
excites me, all those
reserves suggested, though I do hope
that isn't a prosthetic device
under your glove is it?'

'Let's fuck,' he said.

She snuggled close, zipping
him open, unbuckling away
till he lay before her
                  a very
Mars unhorsed but
not doing much of
anything without his horse.

'Strange,' she said, 'you
are still encased in your
defence. You have
a hard cock but there is
something like the

[280]

obduracy of leather
still in your countenance
and your skin, it is like
a hide under hide.'
Then she laid the fierce
pale river of her body
against his, squashing
her lily breasts against
his hard male nipples, inserting
her thighs between his till
he fired a bit and
embracing her with some feeling
moved his head to suck at
the nearest flesh to
his mouth which turned out
to be his own arm.

Then a tremor passed
through his body, the sheen
fell from him, he
became wholly sensitive
as if his body had
rolled back its own foreskin.
(He began to sweat.)

And they melted one
into the other
                    forthwith
like the way the Saône
joins the Rhône at Lyon.

3

Autobiography

The sniff of the real, that's
what I'd want to get
     how it felt
to sit on Parliament
Hill on a May evening
studying for exams   skinny
seventeen   dissatisfied
     yet sniffing such
a potent air, smell of
grass in heat from
the day's sun

I'd been walking through the damp
rich ways by the ponds
and now lay on the upper
grass with Lamartine's poems

life seemed all
loss, and what was more
I'd lost whatever it was
before I'd even had it

a green dry prospect
distant babble of children
and beyond, distinct at
the end of the glow
St Paul's like a stone thimble

longing so hard to make
inclusions that the longing
has become   in memory
an inclusion

Hampstead: the Horse Chestnut Trees

At the top of a low hill
two stand together, green
bobbings contained within
the general sway. They
must be about my age.
My brother and I
rode between them and
down the hill and the impetus
took us on without pedalling
to be finally braked by
a bit of sullen marsh
(no longer there) where the mud
was coloured by the red-brown
oozings of iron. It
was autumn

        or was it?

Nothing to keep it there, the
smell of leaf in May
sweet and powerful as rutting'
confuses me now, it's all
getting lost, I started
forgetting it even as I wrote.

Forms remain, not the life
of detail or hue
then the forms are lost and
only a few dates stay with you.

But the trees have no sentiments
their hearts are wood
and preserve nothing
                    their
boles get great, they are
embraced by the wind they
rushingly embrace,
they spread outward
and upward
                without regret
hardening tender green
to insensate lumber.

The Road Map

If I saw you liked that dull unhappy boy
and let you be, and did not react
to see you driving off together
to the country on Sundays
                              it was
to make your position indefensible
and, that established,
must not my own lack of blame
survive, copious?
(How can you answer back? You were in the wrong.)

I teased a schoolmaster when I was twelve
until his accumulated rage
was out of proportion to the offence.
Thus, I reasoned, there could be no offence.
My emotions drew up a road map.

Now my mind catches up and looks back.

And wreckages of trust litter the route
each an offence against me.
I gaze back
            in hardened innocence.

The Idea of Trust

The idea of trust, or,
the thief. He
was always around,
'pretty' Jim.
Like a lilac bush or
a nice picture on the wall.
Blue eyes of an
intense vagueness
and the well-arranged
bearing of an animal.
Then one day he
said something!
                he said
that trust is
an intimate conspiracy.

What did that
mean? Anyway next day
he was gone, with
all the money and dope
of the people he'd lived with.

I begin
to understand. I see him
picking through their things
at his leisure, with
a quiet secret smile
choosing and taking,
having first discovered
and set up his phrase to
scramble
that message of
enveloping trust.

He's getting
free. His eyes
are almost transparent.
He has put on
gloves. He fingers
the little privacies of those
who acted as if there
should be no privacy.

They took that
risk.
    Wild lilac
chokes the garden.

Courage, a Tale

There was a Child
who heard from another Child
that if you masturbate 100 times
it kills you.

This gave him pause;
he certainly slowed down quite a bit
and also
      kept count.

But, till number 80,
was relatively loose about it.
There did seem plenty of time left.

The next 18
were reserved for celebrations,
like the banquet room in a hotel.

The 99th time
was simply unavoidable.

Weeks passed.

And then he thought
Fuck it
      it's worth dying for,

and half an hour later
the score rose from 99 to 105.

Behind the Mirror

Once in a dark restaurant I caught the eyes of another,
they stared back at mine with unflagging interest.
Another! no it was my own eyes from a recessed mirror.

I and the reflected self seemed identical twins,
alike yet separate, two flowers from the same plant.

Narcissus glares into the pool: someone glares back.
As he leans over the surface, absorbed, he sees
only the other – he sees the rounded arms,
a hunk of auburn hair tumbled forward, lips parted
in awe, in craving: he stares him
straight in the ravenous eyes
                              and reaches down toward him.

He escapes, he does not escape, he is the same, he is other.
If he drowned himself he would be one with himself.
If he drowned himself he would wash free into the world,
placid and circular, from which he has been withdrawn.
He would at last be of it, deep behind the mirror,
white limbs braided with a current
where both water and earth are part of it,
and would come to rest on a soft dark wave of soil
to root there and stand again
                              one flower,
one waxy star, giving perfume, unreflecting.

The Cherry Tree

In her gnarled sleep it
begins
      though she seems
as unmoving as the statue
of a running man: her
branches caught in a
writhing, her trunk
leaning as if in mid-fall.
When the wind moves
against her grave body
only the youngest twigs
scutter amongst themselves.

But there's something going on
in those twisted brown limbs,
it starts as a need
and it takes over, a need
to push
      push outward
from the centre, to
bring what is not
from what is, pushing
till at the tips of the push
something comes about
                  and then
pulling it from outside
until yes she has them started
tiny bumps
appear at the ends of twigs.

Then at once they're all here,
she wears them like a coat
a coat of babies,
I almost think that she
preens herself, jubilant at
the thick dazzle of bloom,
that the caught writhing has become
a sinuous wriggle of joy
beneath her fleece.
But she is working still
to feed her children,
there's a lot more yet,
bringing up all she can
a lot of goodness from roots

while the petals drop.
The fleece is gone
as suddenly as it came
and hundreds of babies are left
almost too small to be seen
but they fatten, fatten, get pink
and shine among her leaves.

Now she can repose a bit
they are so fat.
                    She cares less
birds get them, men
pick them, human children wear them
in pairs over their ears
she loses them all.

That's why she made them,
to lose them into the world, she
returns to herself,
she rests, she doesn't care.

She leans into the wind
her trunk shines black
with rain, she sleeps
as black and hard as lava.
She knows nothing about babies.

Mandrakes

look for us among those
shy flowers opening
at night only
                    in the
shadow, in the held breath
under oak trees listen for

rootshuffle or is it wind
        you won't find us, we
got small a long time back
we withdrew like the Picts
into fireside tale and rumour

we were terrible in our time
gaunt plants fertilized
by the leachings of hanged men
        knobby frames shrieking and
stumping around the planet

smaller and bushier now
prudent green men moving
in oakshadow or among reed
guardians of the young snake
                    rearing from the water
                    with the head and curving
                    neck of a small dinosaur

we can outwait you for
ever if we need, lounging
leafy arms linked along
some park's path, damp fallen leaves
covering our itch to move

mouths open to the wind
sigh entering the sough
from the distant branches

like a rumour at your fireside

Yoko

All today I lie in the bottom of the wardrobe
feeling low but sometimes getting up
to moodily lumber across rooms
and lap from the toilet bowl, it is so sultry
and then I hear the noise of firecrackers again
all New York is jaggedy with firecrackers today
and I go back to the wardrobe gloomy
trying to void my mind of them.
I am confused, I feel loose and unfitted.

At last deep in the stairwell I hear a tread,
it is him, my leader, my love.
I run to the door and listen to his approach.
Now I can smell him, what a good man he is,
I love it when he has the sweat of work on him,
as he enters I yodel with happiness,
I throw my body up against his, I try to lick his lips,
I care about him more than anything.

After we eat we go for a walk to the piers.
I leap into the standing warmth, I plunge into
the combination of old and new smells.
Here on a garbage can at the bottom, so interesting,
what sister or brother I wonder left this message I sniff.
I too piss there, and go on.
Here a hydrant there a pole
here's a smell I left yesterday, well that's disappointing
but I piss there anyway, and go on.

I investigate so much that in the end
it is for form's sake only, only a drop comes out.

I investigate tar and rotten sandwiches, everything, and go on.

And here a dried old turd, so interesting
so old, so dry, yet so subtle and mellow.
I can place it finely, I really appreciate it,
a gold distant smell like packed autumn leaves in winter
reminding me how what is rich and fierce when excreted
becomes weathered and mild
                                but always interesting
and reminding me of what I have to do.

My leader looks on and expresses his approval.

I sniff it well and later I sniff the air well
a wind is meeting us after the close July day
rain is getting near too but first the wind.

Joy, joy,
being outside with you, active, investigating it all,
with bowels emptied, feeling your approval
and then running on, the big fleet Yoko,
my body in its excellent black coat never lets me down,
returning to you (as I always will, you know that)
and now
        filling myself out with myself, no longer confused,
my panting pushing apart my black lips, but unmoving,
I stand with you braced against the wind.

The Release

And I assemble it as it was when I walked on it,
the street, it's unstable, that's what keeps me going,
the sense of mild but constant risk.

I watch him in my mind, the man I saw,
something odd and off-balance about him:
the forward lifted eyes the forward leaning walk,
his yellowish hair bouncing behind him as he walks,
he is beautiful, eager – maybe speeding a little
– with a constant vague air of slight surprise.

With the same hurrying slouch he turns the corner as he did
and as he did he sits on some house-steps in the sun.
He eases to and fro in his consciousness,
he moves in and out of my poem.

What am I doing to this man in the yellow jacket?
Reading him, pretending he is legible,
thinking I can master what is self-contained.
I know only his outer demeanour, his clothing and his skin,
and presume an inner structure I can never be sure of.
I must return to him as he was,
a shimmering planet sheathed in its own air.

The hair on his shoulders stirring in a light wind
he sits on somebody else's front steps and hugs his knees
and stares glowingly ahead as he plans some slightly stoned
    plan:

he's unpredictable, clean of me
(he never notices me as I stare freely).
I must try to leave him as I found him, and so

as if suddenly resolving something
he suddenly unfixes his eyes, jumps to his feet
and slouches eagerly back to the street he came from.

Breaking Ground

1 *Kent*

Lank potato, darkening
cabbage, tattered raspberry
canes, but the flower beds
so crammed there is
no room for weeds
    fiercely aflame all August
when I sniff at the bergamot
the fruity-sage smell is like
a flower sweating

she's too old now to
dig, too old to move
that barrow of cuttings
by the shed, some
nephew can move it

barrow of cuttings, of
grasses not yet hay, fresh
green of redundant
branch, and nasturtium
only rusted a little at
edges of hot yellow

going down to earth, that's
what I can't accept
her kind hand, her
grey eyes, her voice
intonations I've known
all my life – to be

lost, forgotten in
an indiscriminate mulch, a
humus of no colour

2   *Monterey*
Looking down on the stage
from side-bleachers, my mind heavy

October and high fog
Joan Baez singing
Let It Be, during which
a break comes in the sky

and in the crowd below
detail after detail comes
alive, a repeated
movement of stretching arms,
people all over taking off
their coats and shirts,
patches of flesh-colour
start out from the khaki
and grey background

what flashes of warm
skin, what a blooming
of body
            firm
and everlasting petals

Let it be. It
comes to me at last that
when she dies she
loses indeed
that sweet character, loses
all self, and
is dispersed – but dispersal
means
          spreading abroad:

she is not still contained
in the one person, she
is distributed
through fair warm flesh
of strangers
– some have her touch, some
her eyes, some her
voice, never to be
forgotten: renewed again
and again throughout
one great garden which
is always here.
               Shee
is gonn, Shee is lost,
Shee is found, shee
is ever faire.

The Passages of Joy (1982)

I

Elegy

I can almost see it
Thin, tall, half-handsome
the thin hungry sweetness
of his smile gone
as he makes up his mind
and walks behind the barn
in his thin pointed boots
over the crackling eucalyptus leaves
and shoots himself in the head

Even the terror
of leaving life like that
better than the terror
of being unable to handle it

Though I hardly knew him
I rehearse it again and again
Did he smell eucalyptus last?
No it was his own blood
as he choked on it

They keep leaving me
and they don't
tell me they don't
warn me that this is
the last time I'll be seeing them

as they drop away
like Danny or
slowly estrange themselves

There will be no turn of the river
where we are all reunited
in a wonderful party
the picnic spread
all the lost found
as in hide and seek

An odd comfort
that the way we are always
most in agreement
is in playing the same game
where everyone always gets lost

Adultery

Hot beautiful furless animals
played in a clearing opened by their desire
play climaxing to a transparent rage
that raised them above desire itself
– glimpses of clearing after clearing.

Leaving, she recomposed her face
to look as if she had just come
from the new Bergman movie
(which she had in fact seen before).
By the time she was home she'd done it
and her face was all grown over with expression.
Dedicated to her husband, showing
how interesting it had been, how
innovative, a real breakthrough
(you know how I love you, darling?)
he should see it too it would
change his entire outlook.

She played this little drama. And
she half believed it as she shaped it,
having played it before in the interest
of preserving the lovely house,
its rooms airy with freedoms,
the children going to a progressive school,
grass smoked when there were guests,
and philodendrons growing in slow trust.

Her husband looked at her silently,
she seemed, for a moment, an objective matter,
and in his thoughts he reviewed the drama:
a thicket of good-natured fictions,
not interesting, not
innovative, a real throwback
(you know how bored we are, darling?)
she should see it too it would
change her entire outlook.

Bally *Power Play*

Everybody looks at him playing
the machine hour after hour,
but he hardly raises his gold lashes.
Two fingers move, his hips
lean in almost imperceptibly.
He seldom takes his eyes
from the abstract drama of the ball,
the descent and the reverses
of its brief fortunes. He is
the cool source of all that hurry
and desperate activity, in control,
legs apart, braced arms apart,
seeming alive only at the ends.
His haunches are up against the wood now,
the hard edge which he presses
or which presses him
just where the pelvis begins,
above what in the skeleton
would be no more than a hole.
Bally's drama absorbs him:
amongst the variety and surprise
of the lights, the silver ball
appears, rolls shyly towards him,
meets a wheel of red plastic,
at once bounces away from it,
franticly dashes from side to side
and up and down, it is
trapped, it is released,
it springs to the top again
back to where it entered,

but in the end it must disappear
down the hole at the bottom
– and the fifth act is over
leaving behind it only
the continued inane flickering
of coloured light. Between games
he recognizes me, we chat,
he tells me about broken promises
with a comic-rueful smile
at his need for reassurance,
which is as great as anybody's.
He once told me he never starts
to look for the night's partner
until half an hour before closing time.
The rest is foreplay.

New York

It wasn't ringworm he
explained it was speed
made those blotches all
over his body
        On the catwalk
above the turning wheels, high
on risk
     his luck
and the resources of the body
kept him going we were
balancing
       up there
           all night
grinning and panting
hands black with machine oil
grease monkeys of risk
and those wheels were turning *fast*

I return to a sixth floor
where I am staying: the sun
ordering the untidy kitchen,
even the terraced black circles
in the worn enamel are bright,
the faucet dripping,
the parakeets chirping quietly
domestic about their cage,
my dear host in the bed and
his Newfoundland on it, together
stretching, half-woken, as
I close the door.

I calm down,
undress, and slip
in between them and think
of household gods.

The Conversation

You pursue the matter
as yet an edgeless
ghost glimpsed
through a tangle of trees

patient in pursuit
all the long conversation,
answers eliciting further
questions, until you
catch up at last and grasp
the matter tenaciously

though it writhe and slither
and change its shape

– it becomes a flame,
but you hold on,
it becomes a stream,
a struggling fish, a heap
of bones, a soap opera,
and you hold on

your talk defines
bit by bit what
it is indeed about, you
grope for the problematical
life of it
      attracted
to the stirrings, the warmth
like a cat to movement

pinpointing, identifying
the pulse of the matter,
so as to shape from
that flickering life
both what is
and what might be

never perfectly defined
never perfect matter
because the words are
fluent, are fluid
replaced, displaced,
overlapping like
currents of flame or water

stopped at last only
by exhaustion or
arbitrary interruption
Good Night, Good
Night, but in
the cold of the night
in the dark bedroom
the elusive matter
floats above your face
like a faint ectoplasm
milky, amoebic, its
wavering existence drawn
from each outbreathing

from the sleeping head

Expression

For several weeks I have been reading
the poetry of my juniors.
Mother doesn't understand,
and they hate Daddy, the noted alcoholic.
They write with black irony
of breakdown, mental institution,
and suicide attempt, of which the experience
does not always seem first-hand.
It is very poetic poetry.

I go to the Art Museum
and find myself looking for something,
though I'm not sure what it is.
I reach it, I recognize it,
seeing it for the first time.
An 'early Italian altarpiece'.
The outlined Virgin, her lips
a strangely modern bow of red,
holds a doll-sized Child in her lap.
He has the knowing face of an adult,
and a precocious forelock curling
over the smooth baby forehead. She
is massive and almost symmetrical.
He does not wriggle, nor is he solemn.
The sight quenches, like water
after too much birthday cake.
Solidly there, mother and child
stare outward, two pairs of matching eyes
void of expression.

Selves

to Bill Schuessler

I look round the cluttered
icons of your room:
quilt, photo, stuffed bird.
On one wall, the self-portrait
you laboured at these two years
since you broke with your lover.
The new self. It
nags me with its hard eyes,
its simple gaze. Completing it
freed you, apparently,
to other subjects, for
a dozen new sketches are tacked
on another wall. A nude
lolls on some cushions;
a winding road seen from above
pierces the countryside
with a big S.
           I do miss
what you formerly were,
the vulnerable and tender man
I have dreamed about
three nights running. I suppose
it was an imaginary son
that I held onto during this time
of mess and misunderstanding.
But sons grow up,
imaginary ones as well,
and perpetual children are tedious.
Day after day you

went to the gym
where you lifted toward nothing
and your body kept pace
with the body in the self-portrait
you were painting. You lifted
barbells to lower them, but
at the same time you were learning
to carry the other,
the constant weight, the weight
it is necessary to carry.
You got used to the feel
like a hitchhiker
shifting his knapsack
as he improvises his route
along roads already adjusted
to their terrain. Here in your sketch
the roadway pushes forward
like a glittering unsheathed serpent
that tests with the flicker
of his tongue from
side to side as he advances.
You dare place it in the exact
centre of the page from where
it twists upward with
the strength of its pliancy.
It adapts to the rigid
rocky folds of the mountain's skirt
and the soft slopes of the coast
that it slips between
– agile and tactful! –
sometimes lost in a bend
but coming round again:
a flexile sinewy unchecked

curving line it
narrows into the distance where
it steals at last
right off the top of the paper.

A Waking Dream

They are massing at the bank
on the slippery mud, the only light
leaking from the world behind them.
In the middle of the crowd
not in the front pushing but not laggard
on his way to the grey river,
one figure catches my eye.
I see in a strong glint of light
a thick neck half curtained
by black hair, and the back of a head
that I dare recognize,
though knowing it could be another's.
Fearfully, 'Tony!' I call.
And the head turns: it is indeed his,
but he looks through me and beyond me,
he cannot see who spoke,
he is working out a different fate.

Sweet Things

He licks the last chocolate ice cream
from the scabbed corners of his mouth.
Sitting in the sun on a step
outside the laundromat,
mongoloid Don turns his crewcut head
and spies me coming down the street.
'Hi!' He says it with the mannered
enthusiasm of a fraternity brother.
'Take me cross the street!?' part
question part command. I hold
the sticky bunch of small fingers in mine
and we stumble across. They sell
peaches and pears over there,
the juice will dribble down your chin.
He turns before I leave him,
saying abruptly with the same
mixture of order and request
'Gimme a quarter!?' I
don't give it, never have, not to him,
I wonder why not, and as I
walk on alone I realize
it's because his unripened mind
never recognizes me, me
for myself, he only says hi
for what he can get, quarters to
buy sweet things, one after another,
he goes from store to store, from
candy store to ice cream store to
bakery to produce market, unending
quest for the palate's pleasure. Then

out to panhandle again,
more quarters, more sweet things.

My errands are toothpaste,
vitamin pills and a book of stamps.
No self-indulgence there.
But who's this coming up? It's
John, no Chuck, how
could his name have slipped my mind.
Chuck gives a one-sided smile, he stands
as if fresh from a laundromat,
a scrubbed cowboy, Tom Sawyer
grown up, yet stylish, perhaps
even careful, his dark hair
slicked back in the latest manner.
When he shakes my hand I feel
a dry finger playfully bending inward
and touching my palm in secret.
'It's a long time
since we got together,' says John.
Chuck, that is. The warm teasing
tickle in the cave of our handshake
took my mind off toothpaste,
snatched it off, indeed.
How handsome he is in
his lust and energy, in his
fine display of impulse.
Boldly 'How about now?' I say
knowing the answer. My boy
I could eat you whole. In the long pause
I gaze at him up and down and
from his blue sneakers back to the redawning
one-sided smile. We know our charm.

We know delay makes pleasure great.
In our eyes, on our tongues,
we savour the approaching delight
of things we know yet are fresh always.
Sweet things. Sweet things.

The Cat and the Wind

A small wind
blows across the hedge
into the yard.
The cat cocks her ears
– multitudinous rustling
and crackling all around –
her pupils dwindle
to specks in
her yellow eyes
that stare first upward
and then on every side
unable to single out
any one thing
to pounce on,
for all together
as if orchestrated,
twigs, leaves,
small pebbles, pause
and start and pause
in their shifting,
their rubbing
against each other.

She is still listening
when the wind bustles already
three gardens off.

Small Plane in Kansas

C'mon said the pilot and
the three of us climbed onto
the wing and into the snug plane.
With a short run we took off,
lurched upward, soared,
changed direction, missed a treetop,
and found an altitude.
Silo and wood below us
perfect toys, the field
so close you could see
the nested half-circles
where the tractor had turned in ploughing.

That's how it is in the flying dream,
where I step into a wind
with the seven-league boots of euphoria,
letting go, rising, each
pulse a step. Out there
from the height of self-love
I survey the reduced world.

Mastered by mastering,
I so much belong to the wind
I become of it, a gust
that flows, mindless for ever
along unmarked channel
and wall-less corridor where
the world's invisible currents run,
like symptoms, like remedies.

The Exercise

O uncontrollable . . .

Sad little lake, your
glittering grey and the muted
green of overhanging bough
are fresh in memory as
the soft paralysis that had grown in me.
The wider that adolescent
uncertainty of everything,
the sharper was the beauty of
that horrible little lake
within a wood within a fence
put up by the Surrey commuters.

But when wind took over!
On the shore I became of it,
braced and full, or
it partook of me.
It was like an impulse of freedom,
thing but no thing,
here and nowhere,
known only by result, where
for example it pressed water,
blew back trees on the shore,
or combed the long grasses.
I straightened up, facing it,
it seemed a kind of certainty
that I took into me with each breath.
The boisterous presence rummaged
at large in the wood, without it
the trees would have lacked

a condition of their growth.
This bough was blown one way
day by day, month by month,
until that was the way it grew,
but springy and tough
from bearing against wind
to stay upright at all.

Though the wind was like
impulse, it was not impulse.
If I was formed by it, I was formed
by the exercise it gave me.
Exercise in stance, and
in the muscle of feeling.
I became robust standing against it,
as I breathed it so gladly.
The trees resisted, stood, and
gradually bent. The deep grass
accepted, bending at once.
I walked from the lake through
the glum shine of the suburban wood.
The wind blew against me till
I tingled with knowledge.
The swiftly changing
played upon the slowly changing.

Hide and Seek

Children play on into
the summer evening, the block
full of excited shouts.
These girls tied a rope
to the lamppost   higher and higher.
Others sing slightly off-key
counting-out songs, and songs
from TV and Sunday school.
Across the street
                    boys and girls
whoosh by on skateboards
that bump to the end of the block.

From trees behind the houses
birds are calling
about the gathering night.
Chicks scramble
among the familiar ordure
loose-clotted in the nest.

In their fathers' gardens
children are hiding
up in orchard trees, seeking
to be lost and found.

Mother comes down
for the youngest
and as the dark thickens
for the oldest too.

Indoors, under a naked bulb,
eight puppies sleep
close against the huge hairy body
of their mother. The bees
have returned to their Queen.
The crescent moon rises
nine-tenths of it still hidden
but imperceptibly moving
below the moving stars
and hugging the earth.

As Expected

Most of his friends, as expected,
went into service. Two
became pilots, swooping over
lush Vietnamese lowland in their bombers,
high on the orgasmic shriek
of Led Zeppelin over the intercom.

Larry chose a slower route.

He was assigned a grubby
roomful of young men sitting around
idle, or idle on their cots.
One who had been high-spirited
earlier, lay in deep sleep
knocked out by thorazine all day.
Their hair was cropped. Some
would have to be hosed down.
Burdens-on-society.

They looked like ninepins.
But he found that none had head-lice
and let them grow their hair.
They started to look
as if they had different names.

A whole night he watched them
till they forgot he was there.
They paid neighbourly visits
bed to bed. One of them
had composed a little tune
made up of three sounds.

One had invented a game
for the fingers of both hands.
Larry watched:
                 if the unteachable
can teach themselves, it follows
they can be taught by others.

One learned to eat without help.
One learned toilet training
for the first time in his nineteen years.

When he came on his shift
they shambled up, poorly co-ordinated,
wild-eyed, and with faces uncomposed.
'Larry! Larry!' they cried out,
they giggled and embraced him,
stumbling like kittens, inarticulate
like tulips bending in a wet wind,
and learning as they went, like humans.

When the testing time was over,
Larry and the pilots went to college.
The young men in the other institution
were given to other keepers: and they were
retarded, unteachable,
                        as expected.

The Menace

an opposition lurks
in the hollows of the cranium, hides
in the next white chamber
of the linked caverns
haunts the brain hunts the sleeper
through stifling passages

guard	father
executioner	angel of death
delivering doctor	judge
cop	castrator

the-one-who-wants-to-get-me

Come out, come out, wherever you are,
come on out of your hiding place,
put on a body, show me a face.

. . . . . .

So, to objectify.
                    He congeals
from what had seemed sheets
of fallen rainwater
on the pavement between stores.

He leaps from the night
fully armed, a djinn
of human stature.

In the flash of his leap
his helmet and sunshades
seem to reflect everything,
to send it back on itself
untouched and unseen.
Both hands hang heavy
gloved for obscure purpose.
There is menace, perhaps cruelty,
in his inert mouth, suggesting,
as it does, merely the latent.

But I stand against him,
and he settles reluctantly
into a perturbed gleam.
Suddenly, by passing headlights,
I can see what he was, clothed
mannequin in a store window.

I am, am I,
the-one-who-wants-to-get-me

       . . .. ..

The quick air of a new street
hits my face, mixed smell
of the meat district —
cobbles and flags thick
with accumulated grease
from slaughtered animals,
almost the sweet smell of a dairy
when the milk is brought in
in pails, to be strained.

Romantics in leather bars
watch the play of light and dark
on the shine of worn wood,
bottles and badboy uniforms,

frame fantasies like the beginnings
of sentences, form opening clauses,
seeking a plausible conjunction
that a sentence can turn on
to compound the daydream.

. . . . . .

In a theatre of reflection
I encounter again
the exemplary figure,
now can see into
the gleam. Eyes
move behind it,
the mouth smiles, the talk
though sparing suggests
an unceasing thick
traffic of feeling.

He is not a real soldier
but a soldier
inducted by himself
into an army of fantasy
and he greets another.

This time the glitter
pulls me after it.
In a little room
we play at large
with the dull idea of the male
strenuous in his limitations.
We play without deceit,
compressing symbol into fetish,
which is as it were
an object vivified
from inside, a lamp
that abruptly wakens desire
in the night,
        we play
with light and dark.

. . . . . .

From imagination's forcing-house
my man produces
surprise after surprise:

the life of meat,
the charm of institutions,
the banquet of milk.

The finest palate feels
moments before tasting it
the charge of semen,
and only afterwards greets
the sweet and salt in one.

. . . . . .

[340]

Gregory Bateson watching dogs at play: 'The playful nip denotes the bite, but it does not denote what would be denoted by the bite.'

'But' is the word that introduces the second, opposing statement into the sentence. It is a conjunction that changes the simple sentence of the first clause into a compound one. The opposition it introduces does not contradict or delete what came before; instead, the whole sentence could be said to turn on it, since it qualifies and extends the meaning of the first clause, which would otherwise be incomplete.

. . . . . .

I picture a drawing room
where a broad-shouldered man
in an evening gown
who outJudys Judy
conquers by parody
the idea of the female
the frivolous bitch in his head
who haunts him and compels him.
By sullying her poise
by inhabiting it
with his desires
and compounding intentions
he partly exorcises
partly possesses her.

. . . . . .

I think it must be
getting light, a sly
gleam touches a shirt
thrown over a chair,
a wind from the river
nips my cheek.

If we have fought
across the fields of absurdity
we have through our cunning
fought a real army whose
perfected barracks are houses
for the beaten and the dulled.

And we sleep at the end
as a couple. I cup
the fine warm back,
broad fleshed shoulder blades.
We gave the menace
our bodies: his arms
were our arms,
his sperm ours.
His terror became
our play.

. . . . . .

Silt settles: windows clear.
The great piers are being searched
by the wind, but their secrets hide
deep in the meshed gleam of the river.

The 'exemplary figure'
strides away, i.e.
a cheerful man in workclothes
stumbles off grinning
'Bye babe gotta get to the job.'

I see as he goes
how admirably the loose
or withholding stuff of his clothing
has adapted to his body, revealing
what he has become.

the-one-who-wants-to-get-me

guard   angel
guardian   delivering

2

Song of a Camera

for Robert Mapplethorpe

I cut the sentence
out of a life
out of the story
with my little knife

Each bit I cut
shows one alone
dressed or undressed
young full-grown

Look at the bits
He eats he cries
Look at the way
he stands he dies

so that another
seeing the bits
and seeing how
none of them fits

wants to add
adverbs to verbs
A bit on its own
simply disturbs

Wants to say
as well as see
wants to say
valiantly

interpreting
some look in the eyes
a triumph mixed up
with surprise

I cut this sentence
look again
for cowardice
boredom pain

Find what you seek
find what you fear
and be assured
nothing is here

I am the eye
that cut the life
you stand you lie
I am the knife

Waitress

At one they hurry in to eat.
Loosed from the office job they sit
But somehow emptied out by it
And eager to fill up with meat.
   Salisbury Steak with Garden Peas.

The boss who orders them about
Lunches elsewhere and they are free
To take a turn at ordering me.
I watch them hot and heavy shout:
   Waitress I want the Special please.

My little breasts, my face, my hips,
My legs they study while they feed
Are not found on the list they read
While wiping gravy off their lips.
   Here Honey gimme one more scoop.

I dream that while they belch and munch
And talk of Pussy, Ass, and Tits,
And sweat into their double knits,
I serve them up their Special Lunch:
   Bone Hash, Grease Pie, and Leather Soup.

Keats at Highgate

A cheerful youth joined Coleridge on his walk
('Loose,' noted Coleridge, 'slack, and not well-dressed')
Listening respectfully to the talk talk talk
Of First and Second Consciousness, then pressed
The famous hand with warmth and sauntered back
Homeward in his own state of less dispersed
More passive consciousness – passive, not slack,
Whether of Secondary type or First.

He made his way toward Hampstead so alert
He hardly passed the small grey ponds below
Or watched a sparrow pecking in the dirt
Without some insight swelling the mind's flow
That banks made swift. Everything put to use.
Perhaps not well-dressed but oh no not loose.

His Rooms in College

All through the damp morning he works, he reads.
The papers of his students are interrupted
Still by the raw fury, the awkward sadness
His marriage has become. The young serious voices
Are drowned by her remembered piteous wail
'Discovering' the one unfaithfulness
He never did commit.
                    Be more specific.
What do they have ahead of them, poor dears,
This kind of thing?
                    Today no supervisions;
But though he meant these hours for his research
He takes a book, not even in his 'field',
And some note touches him, he goes on reading
Hours long into the afternoon from which
The same low river fog has never lifted.
If every now and then he raises his eyes
And stares at winter lawns below, each time
He sees their hard blurred slopes the less. He reads,
He reads, until the chapel clock strikes five,
And suddenly discovers that the book,
Unevenly, gradually, and with difficulty,
Has all along been showing him its mind
(Like no one ever met at a dinner party),
And his attention has become prolonged
To the quiet passion with which he in return
Has given himself completely to the book.
He looks out at the darkened lawns, surprised
Less by the loss of grief than by the trust.

June

In these two separate rooms we sit,
I at my work, you at yours.
I am at once buried in it
And sensible of all outdoors.

The month is cool, as if on guard,
High fog holds back the sky for days,
But in their sullen patch of yard
The Oriental Poppies blaze.

Separate in the same weather
The parcelled buds crack pink and red,
And rise from different plants together
To shed their bud-sheaths on the bed,

And stretch their crumpled petals free,
That nurse the box of hardening seed,
In the same hour, as if to agree
On what could not have been agreed.

Another All-Night Party

Another all-night party over.
Another night of passages,
Stairs, and angelic messages.
Each cupboard in the back led through
To where the style of dance was new.
One there was rumoured with his lover.

The basement sunk beneath it all
Was watered by a living stream,
As from a grand prophetic dream,
The puddles candling in reflection.
Startled, I almost lost direction
In that wet purgatorial hall.

The drugs wear off, my friend and I
Head for the sidewalks of the day.
Fifth Street at 7 a.m. in May.
So this is where the night-stream led:
Pavements as empty as my head,
Stone city under pale blue sky.

Whereas the night was charged and dense
Now spire and tower piece out the blue.
We laugh, and once more we've run through
Historic night to simpler dawn.
Though even the street we walk upon
Might sparkle with a difference.

I stretch, almost too tired to think,
Cool as a hand freed from a glove
That it began to feel part of,
It had been on so long. We greet
Two other guests on Market Street
And hit the Balcony for a drink.

San Francisco Streets

I've had my eye on you
    For some time now.
You're getting by it seems,
    Not quite sure how.
But as you go along
    You're finding out
What different city streets
    Are all about.

Peach country was your home.
    When you went picking
You ended every day
    With peach fuzz sticking
All over face and arms,
    Intimate, gross,
Itching like family,
    And far too close.

But when you came to town
    And when you first
Hung out on Market Street
    That was the worst:
Tough little group of boys
    Outside Flagg's Shoes.
You learned to keep your cash.
    You got tattoos.

Then by degrees you rose
    Like country cream –
Hustler to towel boy,

Bath house and steam;
Tried being kept a while –
    But felt confined,
One brass bed driving you
    Out of your mind.

Later on Castro Street
    You got new work
Selling chic jewelry.
    And as sales clerk
You have at last attained
    To middle class.
(No one on Castro Street
    Peddles his ass.)

You gaze out from the store.
    Watching you watch
All the men strolling by
    I think I catch
Half-veiled uncertainty
    In your expression.
Good looks and great physiques
    Pass in procession.

You've risen up this high –
    How, you're not sure.
Better remember what
    Makes you secure.
Fuzz is still on the peach,
    Peach on the stem.
Your looks looked after you.
    Look after them.

The Miracle

'Right to the end, that man, he was so hot
That driving to the airport we stopped off
At some McDonald's and do you know what,
We did it there. He couldn't get enough.'
— 'There at the counter?' — 'No, that's public stuff:

'There in the rest room. He pulled down my fly,
And through his shirt I felt him warm and trim.
I squeezed his nipples and began to cry
At losing this, my miracle, so slim
That I could grip my wrist in back of him.

'Then suddenly he dropped down on one knee
Right by the urinal in his only suit
And let it fly, saying Keep it there for me,
And smiling up. I can still see him shoot.
Look at that snail-track on the toe of my boot.'

— 'Snail-track?' — 'Yes, there.' — 'That was six months ago.
How can it still be there?' — 'My friend, at night
I make it shine again, I love him so,
Like they renew a saint's blood out of sight.
But we're not Catholic, see, so it's all right.'

The Victim

Oh dead punk lady with the knack
Of looking fierce in pins and black,
The suburbs wouldn't want you back.

You wished upon a shooting star
And trusted in your wish as far
As he was famous and bizarre.

The band broke up, its gesture made.
And though the music stopped, you stayed.
Now it was with sharp things he played:

Needles and you, not with the band,
Till something greater than you planned
Opened erect within his hand.

You smiled. He pushed it through your shirt
Deep in your belly, where it hurt.
You turned, and ate the carpet's dirt.

And then not understanding why
He watched out with a heavy eye
The several hours you took to die.

The news was full of his fresh fame.
He O.D.'d, ending up the same.
Poor girl, poor girl, what was your name?

3

Painkillers

The King of rock 'n' roll
grown pudgy, almost matronly,
Fatty in gold lamé,
mad King encircled
by a court of guards, suffering
delusions about assassination,
obsessed by guns, fearing
rivalry and revolt

popping his skin
with massive hits of painkiller

dying at forty-two.

What was the pain?
Pain had been the colours
of the bad boy with the sneer.

The story of pain, of separation,
was the divine comedy
he had translated
from black into white.

For white children too
the act of naming the pain
unsheathed
a keen joy at the heart of it.

Here they are still!
the disobedient
who keep a culture alive
by subverting it, turning
for example a subway
into a garden of graffiti.

But the puffy King
lived on, his painkillers
neutralizing, neutralizing,
until he became
ludicrous in performance.

The enthroned cannot revolt.
What was the pain
he needed to kill
if not the ultimate pain

of feeling no pain?

Slow Waker

I look at the nephew,
eighteen, across the breakfast.
He had to be called and called.
He smiles, but without
conviction. He will not
have tea, oh OK,
if it's no trouble,
he will have tea.

His adult face is brand-new.
Once the newness
clears up and it has got
an expression or two
besides bewilderment
he could be a handsome
devil. He could be
a carpenter, a poet, it's
all possible . . .
impossible. The future
is not a word in his mouth.

That, for him, is the trouble:
he lay in bed caught deep
in the mire between
sleep and awake, neither
alert nor resting,
between the flow of night,
ceaselessly braiding itself,
and the gravelly beach
that our soles have thickened on.

Nobody has ever told him
he is good-looking,
just that his feet smell.

He paces through alien London
all day. Everything
is important and unimportant.
He feeds only by osmosis.
He stares at the glint
and blunt thrust of traffic. He
wants to withdraw.

He wants to withdraw into
a small space, like
the cupboard under the stairs
where the vacuum cleaner is kept,
so he can wait, and doze,
and get in nobody's way.

The Girls Next Door

Laughter of sisters, mingling,
separating, but so alike you
sometimes couldn't tell
which was which,
as in a part-song.
I could hear them from outdoors
over the wall
that separated two gardens,
where the lilac bush on our side
was tattered by the passage
of domestic cats, on their constant
wary patrol through
systems of foliage. And then
late afternoons, the sound
of scales on the piano,
of rudimentary tunes.
Evenings, one of them
would call their cat in,
'poor wandering one', a joke
out of Gilbert and Sullivan.

                                  And again

laughter, two voices
like two hands on a piano,
separate but not at variance,
practice in a sunlit room.

Today, many years later,
the younger of the two
tells me about her divorce.
On the phone last week he said
'I didn't give you
the house for ever,
you know. You could learn
a trade at night school.'
'But,' she exclaims to me,
'I'm forty-nine!'

An hour later, from the next room,
I hear her with one of her sons,
and suddenly her laughter
breaks out, as it used to.
Though she is on her own
– for the other sister
died long ago, in her teens –
it is unchanged, a sweet
high stumble of the voice,
rudimentary tune.

Donahue's Sister

She comes level with him at
the head of the stairs
with a slight, arrogant smile
and an inward look, muttering
some injunction to her private world.
Drunk for four days now.

He's unable to get through.
She's not there to get through to.
When he does get through,
next week, it will all sound
exaggerated. She will apologize as if
all too humanly she has caused him
a minute inconvenience.

That sudden tirade last night,
such conviction and logic
— had she always hated him or
was it the zombie speaking?

Scotch for breakfast,
beer all morning.
Fuelling her private world, in which
she builds her case against the public.
Catching at ends of phrases
in themselves meaningless,
as if to demonstrate how well
she keeps abreast.
                    A zombie,
inaccessible and sodden replacement.

He glances at her, her
body stands light and meatless,
and estimates how high he would have
to lift it to launch it
into a perfect trajectory over
the narrow dark staircase
so that it would land on its head
on the apartment-house mosaic of the hallway
and its skull would break in two
– an eggshell full of alcohol –
leaving, at last, his sister
lying like the garbage by the front door
in a pool of Scotch and beer,
understandably, this time, inaccessible.

At an Intersection

I couldn't take my eyes off
the old woman ranging around,
cursing at random,
she was tethered to crisis
like a mobbed witch:

yes, she looked like that,
like an old peasant witch
out of place anywhere,
even at the intersection
where worldly Market Street
meets the slum of Sixth
– head tied up in a kerchief,
apple cheeks, and long nose
as bright and sharp as Anger.

She was screaming abuse
at two plump young cops
who drove off chuckling
in their upholstered police car.
Rambling she cast about
after objects for her rage.
At the bus stop she came against
a young bearded face: it
fixed her with a long pitying look,
which fed her, which fed her.
She discovered an empty pop-bottle,
she danced in front of the traffic
stopped at the red light, waving it,
and smashed it on the asphalt.

Everyone watched, either laughing
or in silent dismay as she flung
her seventy-year-old body about
with the strength of a baby just weaned.

Another time, in his room,
a certain man said to me,
'Please don't be upset
by what I am going to do.
It has nothing to do with you.'
And where he lay he pulled
a pillow over his face
and roared into it several times
– long muffled belches of rage –
as if his trouble was
a sudden cramp or attack
of indigestion to be got rid of
sensibly, by learned measures,

as if it could be
absorbed in the neutral stuff
of a pillow, or by bystanders
who turn away, laughing,

as if the causes
could be smothered with the cry,
but the causes are forgotten
and the cry returns,

                out of control,

raging about an intersection
where the red light is jammed
and the traffic stopped,

the drivers gazing in discomfort
at an anger
unspent, unspendable.

A Drive to Los Alamos

Past mesas in yellow ruin,
breaking up like everything,

upward to the wide plateau
where the novelist went to school,
at the Ranch School for Boys,
in 1929. And that was
all there had been up there.

(His face 'borrowed flesh',
his imagination disguised
in an implacable suit.)
Somebody asked: were you
considered a sissy?
No, he said
in his quiet voice, I was neither
popular nor unpopular.

(The twenty-five boys
of that expensive spartan school
laconic on horses
hunted among the burnt-out furnaces
of the wildness. Where
the rock fell it stayed.)

One building remained, massive
and made of good brown wood,
surrounded now by shoddy
prefab suburb – a street
named after Oppenheimer,
another Trinity Drive.

In the Science Museum
we looked through a brochure
for the extinct school.
That was Mr So-and-so, he said.
That was the infirmary, that was
where the lucky boys went.
(Aware, quietly, of what the past
becomes, golden in ruin.)
Those were the sleeping porches.
Yes, they were cold.
Another picture showed a healthy boy
after a hunt, with the dead deer.
That was Jack Matthews.
(I make up the name,
since I do not remember it,
but he did.)

Transients and Residents

a sequence interrupted

'Albert Hotel,
Transients and Residents'
— NEW YORK, 1970

'Time hovers o'er, impatient to destroy,
And shuts up all the Passages of Joy.'
SAMUEL JOHNSON
'THE VANITY OF HUMAN WISHES'

Falstaff

I always hope to find you circling here
Round the bar's table, playing your old game,
In one hand pool cue, in the other beer.
Vast in your foul burnoose, you'd be the same:
Bullying your little entourage of boys
– Goodlooking but untrustworthy – and later
Ordering them home where, turning up the noise,
You'd party through the night. Neighbourhood satyr,
Old friend, for years you bullied all of us
And did so, you were sure, for our own good.
You took no notice if we made a fuss
Or didn't enjoy ourselves the way we should.
I think of one place you were living at
And all the parties that you used to throw
(That must be when you wore a feathered hat,
Several burnooses, so to speak, ago);
You cooked each evening for some twenty heads,
Not just for streetboys then, for everyone
Who came in want of food or drugs or beds.
The bonus was your boisterous sense of fun.

And though as years have passed your bullying love
Became more desperate (sometimes indeed
Stripped by a ruthlessness you weren't above
It showed itself more nakedly as need);
And though the parties that you gave took place
In other people's houses now, until
They kicked you out for taking all the space;
And though the drugs themselves got questionable –
Too many evenings in the bar have passed
Full of mere chatter and the pumping sound
Of disco on the jukebox since you last
Roared down it for next player or next round.

If you are sick – that's what they say in here
Almost as if by way of an excuse –
The cancer must have rendered you, my dear,
Damnably thin beneath the foul burnoose.

Crystal

He arrives, and makes deliveries, after 3:00,
Then strolls to a ramp that leads up from the dance,
And sits apart, quiet, hands clasped round a knee,
Smelling the fresh-sawed planks, no doubt. Not tense –
Fixed, merely. While he watches us, his face
Is almost readable, his recessed shape
Gleams like a friendly visitor's from space.
As in a sense it is, now. To escape
The sheer impurity of the other lives,
He has always been extreme, he puts his soul
Into each role in turn, where he survives
Till it is incarnation more than role.
Now it is Dealer. 52, tall, scarred,
His looks get nobler every year, I find,

Almost heroic.
                    I once saw in the yard
A half-grown foxglove that he brings to mind
Here, so magnificently self-enwrapped.
Its outer leaves were toothed and all alike.
With a rough symmetry they overlapped
Circling around the budded central spike,
Still green. Dense with its destiny, it waited
Till it might fling itself up into flower.

Now he sits similarly concentrated,
And edged, and similarly charged with power,
Certain of that potential, which his mood
Fairly feeds on, but which is still contained.

The foxglove flowers in its damp solitude
Before its energy fades, and in the end
The chemical in the man will fade as well.
Meanwhile he watches how the dancing feet
Move to the rhythms of the fresh wood-smell;
Inside the crowded night he feels complete.

Crosswords

Your cup of instant coffee by the bed
Cold as the sixties . . . and you chat with me.
For days your excellent strict mind has fed
Only on crossword puzzles and TV.
Though the least self-indulgent man I know
You lie propped up here like an invalid
Pursuing your recuperation, slow,
Relentless, from the world you used to need.
You have seen reason to remove your ground
Far from the great circle where you toiled,

Where they still call their wares and mill around
Body to body, unpausing and unspoiled.
You smell of last week. You do not move much.
You lay your things beside you on the bed
In a precarious pile one sudden touch
Would bring down on you: letters read and reread,
Pens, opera programmes, cigarettes and books.
I think you disturb nothing but the mind.
There: I catch one of those familiar looks
Of thinking through. You reach, you almost find.
Beneath a half-frown your eyes concentrate,
Focussed on what you saw or dreamt you saw,
Alight with their attentiveness, and wait.
Yes, you are active still, you can't withdraw.

Now we take up again the much-discussed
The never-settled topics, (a) change, (b)
Limits of judgment, and of course (c) trust.
We talk, explore, agree and disagree.
. . . I think that you just put me in the wrong.
You want to win, old jesuit. So do I.
You never liked it easy for too long.
I once found that this bed on which you lie
Is just a blanket-covered length of board.
For you, hardness authenticates, and when
Things get too easy, well you make them hard.
. . . We compromise. Then off we go again,
On our renewed cross-country walking tour,
Off with a swinging stride uphill. Stop, though,
Before there's time to disagree once more.
I want to tell you what you no doubt know:

How glad I am to be back at your school
Where it's through contradictions that I learn.
Obsessive and detached, ardent and cool,
You make me think of rock thrown free to turn
At the globe's side, both with and not with us,
Keeping yourself in a companionable
Chilled orbit by the simultaneous
Repulsion and attraction to it all.

Interruption
Though ready in my chair I do not write.
The desk lamp crook'd above me where I lean
Describes a circle round me with its light
– Singling me out; the room falls back unseen.
So, my own island. I can hear the rain
Coming on stealthily, and the rustle grows
Into a thin taptapping on the pane
I stare against, where my reflection glows.

Beyond by day shows that damp square of earth
On which I act out my experiments
– Sowing a seed and watching for the birth:
A tiny pair of leaves, pale rudiments
That might in time grow stronger to assume
A species' characteristics, till I see
Each fresh division soaring into bloom,
Beauty untouched by personality.

My mind shifts inward from such images.
What am I after – and what makes me think
The group of poems I have entered is
Interconnected by a closer link

Than any snapshot album's?
                                    I can try
At least to get my snapshots accurate.
(The thought that I take others' pictures, I,
Far too conceited to find adequate
Pictures they take of me!) Starting outside,
You save yourself some time while working in:
Thus by the seen the unseen is implied.
I like loud music, bars, and boisterous men.
You may from this conclude I like the things
That help me if not lose then leave behind,
What else, the self.
                          I trust the seedling wings,
Yet taking off on them I leave to find.

I find what? In the letters that I send
I imitate unconsciously the style
Of the recipients: mimicking each friend,
I answer expectations, and meanwhile
Can analyse, or drawl a page of wit,
And range, depending on the friend addressed,
From literary to barely literate.
I manage my mere voice on postcards best.

My garden is the plants that I have got
By luck, skill, purchase, robbery, or gift.
From foxglove, lily, pink, and bergamot
I raise leafed unity, a blossoming drift
Where I once found weed waiting out a drought.
But this side of the glass, dry as at noon,
I see the features that my lamp picks out –
Colourless, unjoined, like a damaged moon.

Talbot Road

(where I lived in London 1964–5)

in memory of Tony White

I

Between the pastel boutiques
of Notting Hill and the less defined
windier reaches of the Harrow Road,
all blackened brick, was the street
built for burghers, another Belgravia,
but eventually fallen
to labourers ('No Coloured or Irish
Need Apply') and then like the veins
of the true-born Englishman
filling with a promiscuous mix:
Pole, Italian, Irish, Jamaican,
rich jostling flow. A Yugoslav restaurant
framed photographs of exiled princes,
but the children chattered with a London accent.
I lived on Talbot Road
for a year. The excellent room
where I slept, ate, read, and wrote,
had a high ceiling, on the borders
stucco roses were painted blue.
You could step through the window
to a heavy balcony and even
(unless the drain was blocked)
sup there on hot evenings.
That's what I call complete access –
to air, to street, to friendship:
for, from it, I could see, blocks away,
the window where Tony, my old friend,

toiled at translation. I too tried
to render obscure passages into clear English,
as I try now.

2

Glamorous and difficult friend,
helper and ally. As students
enwrapt by our own romanticism,
innocent poet and actor we had posed
we had played out parts to each other
I have sometimes thought
like studs in a whorehouse.
– But he had to deal
with the best looks of his year.
If 'the rich are different from us',
so are the handsome. What
did he really want? Ah that question . . .

Two romances going on in London,
one in Northampton, one in Ireland,
probably others. Friends and lovers
all had their own versions of him.
Fantastical duke of dark corners,
he never needed to lie:
you had learned not to ask questions.

The fire of his good looks.
But almost concealed by the fringe of fire,
behind the mighty giving of self,
at the centre of the jollity, there was
something withheld, slow, something –
what? what? A damp smoulder of discontent.
He would speculate about 'human relations'

which we were supposed to view
– *vide* Forster, *passim*, etc. –
as an end, a good in themselves.
He did not find them so.

Finally it came to this,
the poses had come undone so far:
he loved you more for your faults
than for anything you could give him.
When once in a pub I lost my temper,
I shouldered my way back from the urinal
and snapped, 'I was too angry to piss.'
The next day he exclaimed with delight,
'Do you know that was the first time
you have ever been angry with me?'
As some people wait for a sign of love,
he had waited how many years
for a sign of anger,
for a sign of other than love.

3
A London returned to after twelve years.
On a long passage between two streets
I met my past self lingering there
or so he seemed
a youth of about nineteen glaring at me
from a turn of desire. He held his look
as if shielding it from wind.
Our eyes parleyed, then we touched
in the conversation of bodies.
Standing together on asphalt openly,
we gradually loosened into a shared laughter.
This was the year, the year of reconciliation

to whatever it was I had come from,
the prickly heat of adolescent emotion,
premature staleness and self-contempt.
In my hilarity, in my luck,
I forgave myself for having had a youth.

I started to heap up pardons
even in anticipation. On Hampstead Heath
I knew every sudden path from childhood,
the crooks of every climbable tree.
And now I engaged these at night,
and where I had played hide and seek
with neighbour children, played as an adult
with troops of men whose rounds intersected
at the Orgy Tree or in the wood
of birch trunks gleaming like mute watchers
or in tents of branch and bush
surrounded by the familiar smell
of young leaf – salty, explosive.
In a Forest of Arden, in a summer night's dream
I forgave everybody his teens.

4

But I came back, after the last bus,
from Hampstead, Wimbledon, the pubs,
the railway arches of the East End,
I came back to Talbot Road,
to the brick, the cement Arthurian faces,
the area railings by coal holes,
the fat pillars of the entrances.
My balcony filled up with wet snow.
When it dried out Tony and I
would lunch there in the sunshine

on veal-and-ham pie, beer, and salad.
I told him about my adventures.
He wondered aloud if he would be happier
if he were queer like me.
How could he want, I wondered,
to be anything but himself?
Then he would have to be off,
off with his jaunty walk,
where, I didn't ask or guess.

At the end of my year, before I left,
he held a great party for me
on a canal boat. The party slipped
through the watery network of London,
grid that had always been glimpsed
out of the corner of the eye
behind fences or from the tops of buses.
Now here we were, buoyant on it,
picnicking, gazing in mid-mouthful
at the backs of buildings, at smoke-black walls
coral in the light of the long evening,
at what we had suspected all along
when we crossed the bridges we now passed under,
gliding through the open secret.

5

That was fifteen years ago.
Tony is dead, the block where I lived
has been torn down. The mind
is an impermanent place, isn't it,
but it looks to permanence.
The street has opened and opened up
into no character at all. Last night

I dreamt of it as it might have been,
the pavement by the church railings
was wet with spring rain,
it was night, the streetlamps' light
rendered it into an exquisite etching.
Sentimental postcard of a dream,
of a moment between race-riots!

But I do clearly remember my last week,
when every detail brightened with meaning.
A boy was staying with (I would think)
his grandmother in the house opposite.
He was in his teens, from the country perhaps.
Every evening of that week
he sat in his white shirt at the window
– a Gothic arch of reduced proportion –
leaning on his arms, gazing down
as if intently making out characters
from a live language he was still learning,
not a smile cracking his pink cheeks.
Gazing down
at the human traffic, of all nations,
the just and the unjust, who
were they, where were they going,
that fine public flow at the edge of which
he waited, poised, detached in wonder
and in no hurry
before he got ready one day
to climb down into its live current.

Night Taxi

for Rod Taylor
wherever he is

Open city
uncluttered as a map.
I drive through empty streets
scoured by the winds
of midnight. My shift
is only beginning and I am fresh
and excitable, master of the taxi.
I relish my alert reflexes
where all else
is in hiding. I have
by default it seems
conquered me a city.

My first address: I
press the doorbell, I lean back
against the hood, my headlights
scalding a garage door, my engine
drumming in the driveway,
the only sound on the block.
There the fare finds me
like a date, jaunty,
shoes shined, I am
proud of myself, on my toes,
obliging but not subservient.

I take shortcuts, picking up
speed, from time to time
I switch on the dispatcher's
litany of addresses,
China Basin to Twin Peaks,
Harrison Street to the Ocean.

I am thinking tonight
my fares are like affairs
— no, more like tricks to turn:
quick, lively, ending up
with a cash payment.
I do not anticipate a holdup.
I can make friendly small talk.
I do not go on about Niggers,
women drivers or the Chinese.
It's all on my terms but
I let them think it's on theirs.

Do I pass through the city
or does it pass through me?
I know I have to be loose,
like my light embrace of the wheel,
loose but in control
— though hour by hour I tighten
minutely in the routine,
smoking my palate to ash,
till the last hour of all
will be drudgery, nothing else.

I zip down Masonic Avenue,
the taxi sings beneath the streetlights
a song to the bare city, it is
my instrument, I woo with it,
bridegroom and conqueror.

I jump out to open the door,
fixing the cap on my head
to, you know, firm up my role,
and on my knuckle
feel a sprinkle of wet.

Glancing upward I see
high above the lamppost
but touched by its farthest light
a curtain of rain already blowing
against black eucalyptus tops.

Poems from the 1980s

Fennel

High fog, white sky
Above me on the bouldered hill
Where I
Stumble between head-high
And scattered clumps of weed
– Fennel, of which I once thought seed
Made you invisible.
Each forms a light green mist
– Feathery auras, though the look deceives,
For looked at closely they consist
Of tiny leading into tinier leaves
In which each fork is sharply separate.
Yet tender, touched: I pinch a sprig and sniff,
And it reminds me of
The other times I have pinched fennel sprigs
For this fierce poignancy.
I stand here as if lost,
As if invisible on this broken cliff,
Invisible sky above.
And for a second I float free
Of personality, and die
Into my senses, into the unglossed
Unglossable
Sweet and transporting yet attaching smell
– The very agent that releases me
Holding me here as well.

Venetian Blind

I pull it down while glancing through
Into my neighbour's room next door:
He being downhill by half a floor
It is his haircut that I view.
Often he greets me on the street
From tennis, or from basketball,
But now he won't look up at all
Frying and sitting down to eat.

You know I'm watching. How I wish
You'd come up here, dark sportive sport.
You'd have more fun than on the court,
And more than with that plate of fish.
You in your sweater with the stripe
In the correct clothes straight from play!
You, resolutely turned away,
Wiping the lips I'd like to wipe!

I study possibility
Through rigid slats, or ordered verses,
Within which border it rehearses
Its partial being, freeing me
Slightly adjusting them to scan
The self-possession that is you,
Who cannot guess at what I do
Here, light-sliced, with another man.

A Bulletin from the Stadium

Lights up on the living
where the boy and girl
stood not islanded
by their embrace but like
a separate district
of the applause
                slick
with the sweat of music
                new-delivered

having pushed against
limits – oh, many years,
and then, suddenly,
after those futile efforts
danced
             with what ease
clear through

obdurate boundaries

kicked away
like the trestles
that hold a crowd in

Reborn into
the shine
of astonished flesh

where they had fallen
headlong, glad
it was unsettled
and irregular, glad too
the new barriers of
clasping bone
were quilted with it

Meat on the bone
meat on the bone
        meat
for the embrace
          there
to discover
and recover
the re
    covered

Smoking Pot on the Bus

what, now, in the eighties!
yet a light vexed whiff
noticeably was travelling up
the bus till the driver
brisk in brown uniform
jumped up, came to
them in the back, told them
temperately, fairly,
'Throw away that joint'
so they did
the ones, there, those
prickly-looking

eyes gone lazy now

the blond's affable drawl
of 'That was a happy
guy why he could have
had the bus surrounded'

in his comfort
edging but not becoming
euphoria, all he wants
the comfort of others

that smoldering ash
promoting virtue

Fighters snort coke
with their whiskey, the one
as easy to buy as the other,
fashionable now
a blade in-turned and out-,
not like these two
who would smilingly
nuzzle the driver
for his justice in an
unkind time, like good
dogs loose and affectionate

'1975'

If to dance the hotel ballroom
is to circle inside a huge untidy kiss,
what must it not be for the desk clerk
who is never seen out of his wet suit,
somber Bodyglove? It must be
like waltzing inside a condom.

An attractive thought. But unfeasible. Rather,
I would coast the hotel-corridors
looking for drug-and-wrestling buddies.
Each room a discrete image,
as in the Cocteau movie of the poet,
or the Kubrick movie of the spooks,
or the Poems of Catullus.
A barracks, a nursery.

Afterwards, I return to Lesbia's floor.
I've bunked in Freedom Hotel so long
I need the pain for stability.
One day I get tired of her:
nothing is unfamiliar any longer,
nothing, it could as well be incest.

I am really *firm*:
       Tough shit, bad lady.
       In the eighties, I shall use
       a pocket calculator for the kisses.

1987

Punch Rubicundus

You give quite a party, old Cocky.
Garden follies, vaudeville of the sexual itch.
I look for the thick smooth hermae
painted red and engorged with racial codings,
a lake of pale green spikes rippling round them.

The surprises of age are no surprise. I am
like one who lurks at a urinal all afternoon,
with a distant look studying younger males
as if they were problems in chess.
But this *can't* be Byzantium. (Though
they do say Uncle Willie's ghost got an invite.)

Here comes our host: hello Mr Punch!
astride a donkey, your prick rampant
– you tilt back to balance your torso against it –
it's big as an inverted cello and much heavier
and requires the assistance of a nymph
to steady it, fingers like bearded barley.

You never had pretty plumage. You knew,
always, that a hard cock was hilarious,
as every schoolboy knows
                              (in lunch hours
riffling through fifty years of allowable jokes
in plum-bound volumes of *Punch*,
ranged like the urinals in Byzantium).

At the Barriers

(Dore Alley Fair)
in memory Robert Duncan

The fog burns off and the crowd mingles promiscuously,
they gaze at each other with a lazy desire
– the whole city block, its trade suspended for today,
is warmed by the sun and by this prolonged friendly lust
that envelops us like an atmosphere, a perfume of the place.
If trade is suspended and this is a holiday
it does not mean that the real business of life is suspended:
in holidays the real business is most engaged.
We wake drowsily to ourselves, we yawn, we stretch,
we stretch our sympathies, this is a day of *feeling with*,
we circulate, we greet our friends, converse in groups,
the competitive spirit is stifled;
in small beginnings our varied loves are based.

. .   . . . .

On the TV screen I saw two Leopard Slugs mating.
They are hermaphroditic, equally taking and giving,
overspread with a pattern of uneven spots, leopard-like.
By a strong thread of mucus reaching from their tails,
which suspends them from a branch of the Tree,
they hang – in air – nothing impeding them
as they twine upon one another, each body
wrapped at every point about the other, twisting in embrace,
in a long slow unstopped writhing of desire,
wholly devoted to the sensual ecstasy.
Glistening, they exude juices from their mutual pressure.

. .   . . . .

Think of the store-rooms and warehouses on this block,
crates stacked here, a dolly propped beneath a smudged
    curtainless window,
a pervasive smell of cardboard, or wood, or metal.
It is a holiday, a Sunday, and the businesses are closed;
but for us in this fair, when we see their signs over doors and
    showrooms,
there are still remembrances of competition.
And we are not as simple as Leopard Slugs,
not hanging in the air we enjoy a sense of impediment,
our amity has an edge, as this atmosphere of loving play
has its limits, each end of the block, marked by flimsy barriers.
All this good will seems easy, but it is set apart
and is a concentration, breathing beside our knowledge of the
    excluded,
on this warming afternoon with the fog in retreat to the ocean.

                    . .   . .   . .

We enter the alley's door
to the party, the music, the drift of laughter and conversation,
we mingle with the jeunesse dorée, we enter the Fair's embrace
of men attracted by men and of women attracted by women,
all together, though there are mixed couples too, all are
    welcome,
for it is an open place, once you have found the way in, like the
    field
where the poet and lover are active, an Arcady of tarmac;
but there must be complication and conflict, humans cannot
    get by without them,
black boots on the black street making a show, a play,
a play of strength, a show of power put on to be disarmed
through the lingering dénouement of an improvised masque

in which aggressiveness reveals its true face as love,
its body as love at play.

. . .. ..

I think of Duncan's Field, trembling grass and middenheap,
where the children dance, clockwise and counterclockwise.
Here between the barriers, the teams of youth and beauty are
    met,
and here the paunchy, dewlapped, and wrinkled, we too
enter this Arcady of a summer's day, and find we have full
    rights here,
and anyone who chooses may come in past the barriers,
the invisible light that exudes from the crowd investing each
    member of it.

The short bartender at the beer-stall works briskly,
his chaps bright with splashes of beer from the cans he opens.
A few feet from me two women embrace, with joking
    boisterous cries.
One of my friends has got so fat I do not recognize him for a
    moment.
A jazz band plays on the stage; there are contests; unarm,
    Eros; I gaze after a young man
of such compacted good looks I can hardly believe it.

Each of us a sum of specifics, each an Arcadian
drawing attention to our difference, our queerness, our shared
    characteristics,
as if this were an Italian-American street fair, or Hispanic, or
    Irish,
but we include the several races and nations, we include the
    temperaments,

the professions, the trades and arts, some of us alcoholic
bums,
our diverse loves subsumed within the general amity,
and 'returning to roots of first feeling'
we play, at the barriers, the Masque of Difference and
Likeness.

The Man with Night Sweats (1992)

I

The Hug

It was your birthday, we had drunk and dined
   Half of the night with our old friend
    Who'd showed us in the end
   To a bed I reached in one drunk stride.
    Already I lay snug,
And drowsy with the wine dozed on one side.

I dozed, I slept. My sleep broke on a hug,
    Suddenly, from behind,
In which the full lengths of our bodies pressed:
    Your instep to my heel,
   My shoulder-blades against your chest.
   It was not sex, but I could feel
   The whole strength of your body set,
    Or braced, to mine,
    And locking me to you
   As if we were still twenty-two
   When our grand passion had not yet
    Become familial.
   My quick sleep had deleted all
   Of intervening time and place.
    I only knew
The stay of your secure firm dry embrace.

To a Friend in Time of Trouble

You wake tired, in the cabin light has filled,
Then walk out to the deck you helped to build,
And pause, your senses reaching out anxiously,
Tentatively, toward scrub and giant tree:
A giving of the self instructed by
The dog who settles near you with a sigh
And seeks you in your movements, following each.
Though yours are different senses, they too reach
Until you know that they engage the air
– The clean and penetrable medium where
You encounter as if they were a sort of home
Fountains of fern that jet from the coarse loam.

You listen for the quiet, but hear instead
A sudden run of cries break overhead,
And look to see a wide-winged bird of prey
Between the redwood tops carrying away
Some small dark bundle outlined in its claws.
The certainty, the ease with which it draws
Its arc on blue . . . Soon the protesting shriek,
The gorging from the breast, the reddened beak,
The steadying claw withdrawn at last. You know
It is not cruel, it is not human, though
You cringe who would not feel surprised to find
Such lacerations made by mind on mind.

Later, the job, you haul large stones uphill.
You intend to pile them in a wall which will,
In front of plantings and good dirt, retain
Through many a winter of eroding rain.
Hard work and tiring, but the exercise
Opens the blood to air and simplifies
The memory of your troubles in the city,
Until you view them unconfused by pity.

A handsome grey-haired, grey-eyed man, tight-knit;
Each muscle clenching as you call on it
From the charmed empire of your middle age.
You move about your chores: the grief and rage
You brought out here begin at last to unbind.
And all day as you climb, the released mind
Unclenches till – the moment of release
Clean overlooked in the access of its own peace –
It finds that it has lost itself upon
The smooth red body of a young madrone,
From which it turns toward other varying shades
On the brown hillside where light grows and fades,
And feels the healing start, and still returns,
Riding its own repose, and learns, and learns.

Bone

It was at first your great
Halo of aureate-
brown curls distracted me.
And it was a distraction
Not from the hard-filled lean
Body that I desired
But from the true direction
Your face took, what it could mean,
Though it was there to see.

When you, that second day,
Drew back the shower curtain,
Another man stood there,
His drowned hair lay
Chastened and flattened down,
And I saw then for certain
How Blackfoot Indian bone
Persisting in the cheek,
The forehead, nape, and crown,
Had underlain the hair,
Which was mere ornament
– A European mock.

Could that be what it meant?
That high unsoftened rock
With no trees on.

An Invitation

from San Francisco
to my brother

Dear welcomer, I think you must agree
   It is your turn to visit me.
I'll put you in my room, sunk far from light,
   Where cars will not drive through your night.
Out of the window you can sneak a look
   To see some jolly neighbours cook
Down in their kitchen, like a lighted box
   Beyond the fence, where over fox-
glove, mint, and ribs of fern, the small dark plain
   Fingers of ivy graze my pane.
(Perhaps before you come I'll snip them off.)
   Once you have rested up enough
We'll bolt our porridge down before it's cool
   As if about to go to school.
But we are grown-up now, and we can go
   To watch the banked Pacific throw
Its rolling punches at a flowered hill
   Where garden seeds were dumped in fill.
Or we can take the Ferry across the Bay
   Scanning the washed views on our way
To Sausalito where the thing to do
   Is look at yet another view
And take the Ferry back. Or we can climb
   To murals from an earlier time:
A chunky proletariat of paint
   In allegorical restraint
Where fat silk-hatted bosses strut and cower

Around the walls inside a tower
Shaped like the nozzle of a fireman's hose.

By then you will have noticed those
Who make up Reagan's proletariat:
    The hungry in their long lines that
Gangling around two sides of city block
    Are fully formed by ten o'clock
For meals the good Franciscan fathers feed
    Without demur to all who need.
You'll watch the jobless side by side with whores
    Setting a home up out of doors.
And every day more crazies who debate
    With phantom enemies on the street.
I did see one with bright belligerent eye
    Gaze from a doorstep at the sky
And give the finger, with both hands, to God:
    But understand, he was not odd
Among the circumstances.
                            Well, I think
    After all that, we'll need a drink.
We may climb hills, but won't tax a beginner
    Just yet, and so come home to dinner
With my whole household, where they all excel:
    Each cooks one night, and each cooks well.
And while food lasts, and after it is gone,
    We'll talk, without a TV on,
We'll talk of all our luck and lack of luck,
    Of the foul job in which you're stuck,
Of friends, of the estranged and of the dead
    Or living relatives instead,
Of what we've done and seen and thought and read,
    Until we talk ourselves to bed.

The Differences

Reciting Adrienne Rich on Cole and Haight,
Your blond hair bouncing like a corner boy's,
You walked with sturdy almost swaggering gait,
The short man's, looking upward with such poise,
Such bold yet friendly curiosity
I was convinced that clear defiant blue
Would have abashed a storm-trooper. To me
Conscience and courage stood fleshed out in you.

So when you gnawed my armpits, I gnawed yours
And learned to associate you with that smell
As if your exuberance sprang from your pores.
I tried to lose my self in you as well.
To lose my self . . . I did the opposite,
I turned into the boy with iron teeth
Who planned to eat the whole world bit by bit,
My love not flesh but in the mind beneath.

Love takes its shape within that part of me
(A poet says) *where memories reside.*
And just as light marks out the boundary
Of some glass outline men can see inside,
So love is formed by a dark ray's invasion
From Mars, its dwelling in the mind to make.
Is a created thing, and has sensation,
A soul, and strength of will.
                                                    It is opaque.

Opaque, yet once I slept with you all night
Dreaming about you – though not quite embraced
Always in contact felt however slight.
We lay at ease, an arm loose round a waist,
Or side by side and touching at the hips,
As if we were two trees, bough grazing bough,
The twigs being the toes or fingertips.
I have not crossed your mind for three weeks now,

But think back on that night in January,
When casually distinct we shared the most
And lay upon a bed of clarity
In luminous half-sleep where the will was lost.
We woke at times and as the night got colder
Exchanged a word, or pulled the clothes again
To cover up the other's exposed shoulder,
Falling asleep to the small talk of the rain.

Lines for My 55th Birthday

The love of old men is not worth a lot,
Desperate and dry even when it is hot.
You cannot tell what is enthusiasm
And what involuntary clawing spasm.

Philemon and Baucis

love without shadows – W.C.W.

Two trunks like bodies, bodies like twined trunks
Supported by their wooden hug. Leaves shine
In tender habit at the extremities.
Truly each other's, they have embraced so long
Their barks have met and wedded in one flow
Blanketing both. Time lights the handsome bulk.
  The gods were grateful, and for comfort given
Gave comfort multiplied a thousandfold.
Therefore the couple leached into that soil
The differences prolonged through their late vigour
That kept their exchanges salty and abrasive,
And found, with loves balancing equally,
Full peace of mind. They put unease behind them
A long time back, a long time back forgot
How each woke separate through the pale grey night,
A long time back forgot the days when each
– Riding the other's nervous exuberance –
Knew the slow thrill of learning how to love
What, gradually revealed, becomes itself,
Expands, unsheathes, as the keen rays explore:
Invented in the continuous revelation.

They have drifted into a perpetual nap,
The peace of trees that all night whisper nothings.

Odysseus on Hermes

his afterthought

I was seduced by innocence
– beard scarcely visible on his chin –
by the god within.
The incompletion of youth
like the new limb of the cactus growing
– soft-green – not fully formed
the spines still soft and living,
potent in potential,
in process and so
still open to the god.
>   When complete and settled
>   then closed to the god.
So sensing it in him
I was seduced by the god,
becoming in my thick maturity
suddenly unsettled
>   un-solid
still being formed –
in the vulnerability, edges flowing,
myself open to the god.

I took his drug
and all came out right in the story.
Still thinking back
I seek to renew that power
so easily got
seek to find again that knack
of opening my settled features,
creased on themselves,
to the astonishing kiss and gift
of the wily god to the wily man.

Seesaw

song

Days are bright,
Nights are dark.
We play seesaw
In the park.

Look at me
And my friend
Freckleface
The other end.

Shiny board
Between my legs.
Feet crunch down
On the twigs.

I crouch close
To the ground
Till it's time:
Up I bound.

Legs go loose,
Legs go tight.
I drop down
Like the night.

Like a scales.
Give and take,
Take and give
My legs ache.

So it ends
As it begins.
Off we climb
And no one wins.

2

A Sketch of the Great Dejection

Having read the promise of the hedgerow
the body set out anew on its adventures.
At length it came to a place of poverty,
of inner and outer famine,
        where all movement had stopped
except for that of the wind, which was continual
and came from elsewhere, from the sea,
moving across unplanted fields and between headstones
in the little churchyard clogged with nettles
where no one came between Sundays, and few then.
The wind was like a punishment to the face and hands.
These were marshes of privation:
the mud of the ditches oozed scummy water,
the grey reeds were arrested in growth,
the sun did not show, even as a blur,
and the uneven lands were without definition
as I was without potent words,
inert.
      I sat upon a disintegrating gravestone.
How can I continue? I asked.
I longed to whet my senses, but upon what?
On mud? It was a desert of raw mud.
I was tempted by fantasies of the past,
but my body rejected them, for only in the present
could it pursue the promise,
        keeping open to its fulfilment.
I would not, either, sink into the mud,
warming it with the warmth I brought to it,
        as in a sty of sloth.

My body insisted on restlessness
                   having been promised love,
as my mind insisted on words
                   having been promised the imagination.
So I remained alert, confused and uncomforted.
I fared on and, though the landscape did not change,
it came to seem after a while like a place of recuperation.

3

Patch Work

The bird book says, common, conspicuous.
This time of year all day
The mockingbird
Sweeps at a moderate height
Above the densely flowering
Suburban plots of May,
The characteristic shine
Of white patch cutting through the curved ash-grey
That bars each wing;
Or it appears to us
Perched on the post that ends a washing-line
To sing there, as in flight,
A repertoire of songs that it has heard
— From other birds, and others of its kind —
Which it has recombined
And made its own, especially one
With a few separate plangent notes begun
Then linking trills as a long confident run
Toward the immediate distance,
Repeated all day through
In the sexual longings of the spring
(Which also are derivative)
And almost mounting to
Fulfilment, thus to give
Such muscular vigour to a note so strong,
Fulfilment that does not destroy
The original, still-unspent
Longings that led it where it went
But links them in a bird's inhuman joy

Lifted upon the wing
Of that patched body, that insistence
Which fills the gardens up with headlong song.

The Life of the Otter

Tucson Desert Museum

From sand he pours himself into deep water,
His other liberty
                in which he swims
Faster than anything that lives on legs,
In wide parabolas
                figures of eight
Long loops
                drawn with the accuracy and ease
Of a lithe skater hands behind her back
Who seems to be showing off
                      but is half lost
In the exuberance of dip and wheel.

The small but long brown beast reaches from play
Through play
                to play
                    play not as relaxation
Or practice or escape but all there is:
Activity   (hunt, procreation, feeding)
Functional but as if gratuitous.

Now
    while he flows
                    out of a downward curve
I glimpse through glass
                  his genitals as neat
As a stone acorn with its two oak leaves
Carved in a French cathedral porch,
                      relief

Exposed
       crisply detailed
              above the sway
Of this firm muscular trunk
                  caught in mid-plunge,
Of which the speed contains its own repose
Potency
       set in fur
           like an ornament.

Three for Children

Cannibal

Shark, with your mouth tucked under
That severs like a knife,
You leave no time for wonder
In your swift thrusting life.

You taste blood. It's your brother's,
And at your side he flits.
But blood, like any other's.
You bite him into bits.

The Aquarium

The dolphins play
Inside their pool all day
And through its bright blue water swing and wheel.
Though on display
They send out on their way
A song that we hear as a long light squeal.

But what they say
Is 'Oh the world is play!
Look at these men we have no cause to thank:
If only they
Would free themselves in play,
As we do even in this confining tank.'

The Seabed

A moray eel lies wound amongst the stone,
Colour of sand, its mouth a level slit.
Of all it snaps up here, and makes its own,
Octopus tentacles are its favourite.
It waits. Although it would not mean to hurt
A human if it met one in this spot,
It has indeed been known, although alert,
To make mistakes, as which of us has not.
For if across the underwater sand
Skindivers sometimes dancingly intrude,
It may confuse the fingers of a hand,
Wriggling through water, for its favourite food.

Skateboard

Tow Head on his skateboard
threads through a crowd
of feet and faces delayed
to a slow stupidity.
Darts, doubles, twists.
You notice how nimbly
the body itself has learned
to assess the relation between
the board, pedestrians,
and immediate sidewalk.
Emblem. Emblem of fashion.
Wearing dirty white
in dishevelment as delicate
as the falling draperies
on a dandyish
Renaissance saint.
Chain round his waist.
One hand gloved.
Hair dyed to show it is dyed,
pale flame spiking from fuel.
Tow Head on Skateboard
perfecting himself:
emblem extraordinary
of the ordinary.

In the sexless face
eyes innocent of feeling
therefore suggest the spirit.

Well Dennis O'Grady

Well Dennis O'Grady
said the smiling old woman
pausing at the bus stop I hear
they are still praying for you
I read it in the Bulletin.

His wattle throat sagged
above his careful tie and clean brown suit.
I didn't hear his answer,
but though bent a bit
over his stick
he was delighted to be out
in the slight December sunshine
– having a good walk, pleased
it seems at all the prayers
and walking pretty straight
on his own.

Outside the Diner

Off garbage outside the diner
he licks the different flavours
of greasy paper like a dog
and then unlike a dog
eats the paper too.

Times are
there's a lethargic
conviviality, as they sit around
a waste lot passing muscatel
which warms each in his sour sheath
worn so long that the smell
is complex, reminiscent
of food cooking or faeces.

Times are
there's the Detox Clinic, times are
he sleeps it off across the back seat
of an auto with four flat tyres,
blackened sole and heel
jammed against the side windows,
bearded face blinded by sleep
turned toward the light.
Another lies on the front seat.

A poor weed,
unwanted scraggle tufted
with unlovely yellow,
persists between paving stones
marginal to the grid
bearded face turned toward light.

Improvisation

I said our lives are improvisation and it sounded
un-rigid, liberal, in short a good idea.
But that kind of thing is hard to keep up:
guilty lest I gave to the good-looking only
I decided to hand him a quarter
whenever I saw him – what an ugly young man:
wide face, round cracked lips, big forehead
striped with greasy hairs. One day he said
'You always come through' and I do, I did,
except that time he was having a tantrum
hitting a woman, everyone moving away,
I pretending not to see, ashamed.
                                        Mostly
he perches on the ungiving sidewalk, shits
behind bushes in the park, seldom weeps,
sleeps bandaged against the cold, curled
on himself like a wild creature,
his agility of mind wholly employed
with scrounging for cigarettes, drugs, drink
or the price of Ding Dongs, with dodging knife-fights,
with ducking cops and lunatics, his existence
paved with specifics like an Imagist epic,
the only discourse printed on shreds of newspaper,
not one of which carries the word improvisation.

Old Meg

dark as a gypsy, berry-
brown with dirt
sticks to the laundromats
in cold weather
                in the sun
sit near her on the bus-bench
and you'll smell something
of dog, something of mould

I've seen her beaming
at concrete 'You didn't make sense
at first I couldn't have known
who you were' Extraterrestrial
friends no doubt
                But to me
venturing once to greet her
she responded with
                    'Blood on you!'

Yellow Pitcher Plant

flowering stomach

scroll of leaf

covered with small honeyed
warts by which the seely fly
is lured to sloping
pastures at the trumpet's lip

till grazing downhill
the fly finds the underbrush
of hairs casually pushed through
has closed behind –
a thicket of lances – sharkteeth –
trap
                  oh alas!
it stumbles on, falling
from chamber to chamber
within the green turret
making each loud
with the buzz of its grief
and finally slipping into
the oubliette itself
– pool that digests protein –

to become mere
chitinous exoskeleton,
leftovers

of a sated petal

an enzyme's cruelty

Tenderloin

This poverty recognizes
a street only as link
between corners greasy
with expedient, corners
turned or waited on
slippery as they may be
for transactions, or news of them.

Not poverty beaten
down, poverty rather
on the make, without being
clever enough to make it.
Smallish sums pass hands.
This poverty seeks out
stereotype: gentle
black whore, foul-mouthed
old cripple, snarling skinhead,
tottering transvestite, etc.
City romantics.
Come on, you,
obey your impulse,
costs only a little more
than in the country.

It's all so
slippery, but
you might say one lubricant
is as good as another.

And there's no such thing
as an insincere
erection is there?

Think of Spanish
Fly, it irritates
the urethra which
has been capable, however,
of responding
to more delicate stimuli.

And of the loins too,
firm open slopes that lead
to the padded valley
Tender loin
protecting the serviceable
channel and glands
delicate almost as
eyeballs – Tender-
ness anaesthetized and irritated

Strip it bare

Grease it well
with its own foul
lubricant

Against the grit
of its own sharp corners
scrape it to orgasm

Looks

Those eyes appear to transmit energy
And hold it back undissipated too.
His gaze is like a star, that cannot see,
A glow so steady he directs at you
You try to be the first to look aside
– Less flattered by the appearance of attention
Than vexed by the dim stirrings thus implied
Within a mind kept largely in suspension.

Although a gaze sought out, and highly placed,
By lovers and photographers, it is
Too patly overwhelming for your taste.
You step back from such mannered solemnities
To focus on his no doubt sinewy power,
His restless movements, and his bony cheek.
You have seen him in the space of one half-hour
Cross a street twenty times. You have heard him speak,
Reading his work to the surprise of guests
Who find that dinner was a stratagem:
Poems in which the attracted turn to pests
If they touch him before he touches them,
In which the celebrant of an appetite
Richly fulfilled will say Get off me bitch
To one who thought she had an equal right
To her desires, – nevertheless in which
He holds you by the voice of his demands,
Which take unfaltering body on the air
As need itself, live, famished, clenched like hands
Pale at the knuckle. Then, his luminous stare,
That too. He is an actor, after all,

And it's a genuine talent he engages
In playing this one character, mean, small,
But driven like Othello by his rages
As if a passion for no matter what,
Even the self, is fully justified,
Or as if anger could repopulate
The bony city he is trapped inside.

At times he has a lover he can hurt
By bringing home the pick-ups he despises
Because they let him pick them up. Alert
Always to looks – and they must look like prizes –
He blurs further distinction, for he knows
Nothing of strength but its apparent drift,
Tending and tending, and nothing of repose
Except within his kindled gaze, his gift.

To Isherwood Dying

It could be, Christopher, from your leafed-in house
In Santa Monica where you lie and wait
    You hear outside a sound resume
      Fitful, anonymous,
    Of Berlin fifty years ago
    As autumn days got late –
The whistling to their girls from young men who
    Stood in the deep dim street, below
Dingy façades which crumbled like a cliff,
    Behind which in a rented room
      You listened, wondering if
By chance one might be whistling up for you,
    Adding unsentimentally
      'It could not possibly be.'
Now it's a stricter vigil that you hold
And from the canyon's palms and crumbled gold
    It could be possibly
    You hear a single whistle call
      Come out
      Come out into the cold.
Courting insistent and impersonal.

Christmas week, 1985

The Stealer

I lie and live
my body's fear
something's at large
and coming near

No deadbolt
can keep it back
A worm of fog
leaks through a crack

From the darkness
as before
it grows to body
in my door

Like a taker
scarved and gloved
it steals this way
like one I loved

Fear stiffens me
and a slow joy
at the approach
of the sheathed boy

Will he too do
what that one did
unlock me first
open the lid

and reach inside
with playful feel
all the better
thus to steal

JVC

He concentrated, as he ought,
On fitting language to his thought
And getting all the rhymes correct,
Thus exercising intellect
In such a space, in such a fashion,
He concentrated into passion.

Barren Leaves

Spontaneous overflows of powerful feeling:
Wet dreams, wet dreams, in libraries congealing.

Jamesian

Their relationship consisted
In discussing if it existed.

.

Meat

My brother saw a pig root in a field,
And saw too its whole lovely body yield
To this desire which deepened out of need
So that in wriggling through the mud and weed
To eat and dig were one athletic joy.
When we who are the overlords destroy
Our ranging vassals, we can therefore taste
The muscle of delighted interest
We make into ourselves, as formerly
Hurons digested human bravery.

Not much like this degraded meat – this meal
Of something, was it chicken, pork, or veal?
It tasted of the half-life that we raise
In high bright tombs which, days, and nights like days,
Murmur with nervous sound from cubicles
Where fed on treated slop the living cells
Expand within each creature forced to sit
Cramped with its boredom and its pile of shit
Till it is standard weight for roast or bacon
And terminated, and its place is taken.

To make this worth a meal you have to add
The succulent liberties it never had
Of leek, or pepper fruiting in its climb,
The redolent adventures dried in thyme
Whose branches creep and stiffen where they please,
Or rosemary that shakes in the world's breeze.

Cafeteria in Boston

I could digest the white slick watery mash,
The two green peppers stuffed with rice and grease
In Harry's Cafeteria, could digest
Angelfood cake too like a sweetened sawdust.
I sought to extend the body's education,
Forced it to swallow down the blunted dazzle
Sucked from the red formica where I leaned.
Took myself farther, digesting as I went,
Course after course: even the bloated man
In cast-off janitor's overalls, who may
Indeed have strayed through only for the toilets;
But as he left I caught his hang-dog stare
At the abandoned platefuls crusted stiff
Like poisoned slugs that froth into their trails.
I stomached him, him of the flabby stomach,
Though it was getting harder to keep down.
But how about the creature scurrying in
From the crowds wet on the November sidewalk,
His face a black skull with a slaty shine,
Who slipped his body with one fluid motion
Into a seat before a dish on which
Scrapings had built a heterogeneous mound,
And set about transferring them to his mouth,
Stacking them faster there than he could swallow,
To get a start on the bus-boys. My mouth too
Was packed, its tastes confused: what bitter juices
I generated in my stomach as
Revulsion met revulsion. Yet at last
I lighted upon meat more to my taste
When, glancing off into the wide fluorescence,

I saw the register, where the owner sat,
And suddenly realized that he, the cooks,
The servers of the line, the bus-boys, all
Kept their eyes studiously turned away
From the black scavenger. Digestively,
That was the course that kept the others down.

Nasturtium

Born in a sour waste lot
You laboured up to light,
Bunching what strength you'd got
And running out of sight
Through a knot-hole at last,
To come forth into sun
As if without a past,
Done with it, re-begun.

Now street-side of the fence
You take a few green turns,
Nimble in nonchalance
Before your first flower burns.
From poverty and prison
And undernourishment
A prodigal has risen,
Self-spending, never spent.

Irregular yellow shell
And drooping spur behind . . .
Not rare but beautiful
— Street-handsome — as you wind
And leap, hold after hold,
A golden runaway
Still running, strewing gold
From side to side all day.

The Beautician

She, a beautician, came to see her friend
Inside the morgue, when she had had her cry.
She found the body dumped there all awry,
Not as she thought right for a person's end,
Left sideways like that on one arm and thigh.

In their familiarity with the dead
It was as if the men had not been kind
With her old friend, whose hair she was assigned
To fix and shape. She did not speak; instead
She gave her task a concentrated mind.

She did find in it some thin satisfaction
That she could use her tenderness as skill
To make her poor dead friend's hair beautiful
— As if she shaped an epitaph by her action,
She thought — being a beautician after all.

'All Do Not All Things Well'

Implies that some therefore
Do well, for its own sake,
One thing they undertake,
Because it has enthralled them.

I used to like the two
Auto freaks as I called them
Who laboured in their driveway,
Its concrete black with oil,
In the next block that year.

One, hurt in jungle war,
Had a false leg, the other
Raised a huge beard above
A huge Hell's Angel belly.

They seemed to live on beer
And corn chips from the deli.

Always with friends, they sprawled
Beneath a ruined car
In that inert but live way
Of scrutinizing innards.
And one week they extracted
An engine to examine,
Transplant shining like tar
Fished out into the sun.

'It's all that I enjoy,'
Said the stiff-legged boy.
That was when the officious
Realtor had threatened them
For brashly operating
A business on the street
– An outsider, that woman
Who wanted them evicted,
Wanted the neighbourhood neat
To sell it. That was when
The boy from Vietnam told me
That he'd firebomb her car.
He didn't of course, she won.

I am sorry that they went.
Quick with a friendly greeting,
They were gentle joky men
– Certainly not ambitious,
Perhaps not intelligent
Unless about a car,
Their work one thing they knew
They could for certain do
With a disinterest
And passionate expertise
To which they gave their best
Desires and energies.
Such oily-handed zest
By-passed the self like love.
I thought that they were good
For any neighbourhood.

4

Rain punishes the city,
like raw mind that batters flesh,
ever saddened by what fails.

Charlie Hinkle

The Man with Night Sweats

I wake up cold, I who
Prospered through dreams of heat
Wake to their residue,
Sweat, and a clinging sheet.

My flesh was its own shield:
Where it was gashed, it healed.

I grew as I explored
The body I could trust
Even while I adored
The risk that made robust,

A world of wonders in
Each challenge to the skin.

I cannot but be sorry
The given shield was cracked
My mind reduced to hurry,
My flesh reduced and wrecked.

I have to change the bed,
But catch myself instead

Stopped upright where I am
Hugging my body to me
As if to shield it from
The pains that will go through me,

As if hands were enough
To hold an avalanche off.

In Time of Plague

My thoughts are crowded with death
and it draws so oddly on the sexual
that I am confused
confused to be attracted
by, in effect, my own annihilation.
Who are these two, these fiercely attractive men
who want me to stick their needle in my arm?
They tell me they are called Brad and John,
one from here, one from Denver, sitting the same
on the bench as they talk to me,
their legs spread apart, their eyes attentive.
I love their daring, their looks, their jargon,
and what they have in mind.

Their mind is the mind of death.
They know it, and do not know it,
and they are like me in that
(I know it, and do not know it)
and like the flow of people through this bar.
Brad and John thirst heroically together
for euphoria – for a state of ardent life
in which we could all stretch ourselves
and lose our differences. I seek
to enter their minds: am I a fool,
and they direct and right, properly
testing themselves against risk,
as a human must, and does,
or are they the fools, their alert faces
mere death's heads lighted glamorously?
I weigh possibilities

till I am afraid of the strength
of my own health
and of their evident health.

They get restless at last with my indecisiveness
and so, first one, and then the other,
move off into the moving concourse of people
who are boisterous and bright
carrying in their faces and throughout their bodies
the news of life and death.

Lament

Your dying was a difficult enterprise.
First, petty things took up your energies,
The small but clustering duties of the sick,
Irritant as the cough's dry rhetoric.
Those hours of waiting for pills, shot, X-ray
Or test (while you read novels two a day)
Already with a kind of clumsy stealth
Distanced you from the habits of your health.

In hope still, courteous still, but tired and thin,
You tried to stay the man that you had been,
Treating each symptom as a mere mishap
Without import. But then the spinal tap.
It brought a hard headache, and when night came
I heard you wake up from the same bad dream
Every half-hour with the same short cry
Of mild outrage, before immediately
Slipping into the nightmare once again
Empty of content but the drip of pain.
No respite followed: though the nightmare ceased,
Your cough grew thick and rich, its strength increased.
Four nights, and on the fifth we drove you down
To the Emergency Room. That frown, that frown:
I'd never seen such rage in you before
As when they wheeled you through the swinging door.
For you knew, rightly, they conveyed you from
Those normal pleasures of the sun's kingdom
The hedonistic body basks within
And takes for granted – summer on the skin,
Sleep without break, the moderate taste of tea
In a dry mouth. You had gone on from me

As if your body sought out martyrdom
In the far Canada of a hospital room.
Once there, you entered fully the distress
And long pale rigours of the wilderness.
A gust of morphine hid you. Back in sight
You breathed through a segmented tube, fat, white,
Jammed down your throat so that you could not speak.
　How thin the distance made you. In your cheek
One day, appeared the true shape of your bone
No longer padded. Still your mind, alone,
Explored this emptying intermediate
State for what holds and rests were hidden in it.
　You wrote us messages on a pad, amused
At one time that you had your nurse confused
Who, seeing you reconciled after four years
With your grey father, both of you in tears,
Asked if this was at last your 'special friend'
(The one you waited for until the end).
'She sings,' you wrote, 'a Philippine folk song
To wake me in the morning . . . It is long
And very pretty.' Grabbing at detail
To furnish this bare ledge toured by the gale,
On which you lay, bed restful as a knife,
You tried, tried hard, to make of it a life
Thick with the complicating circumstance
Your thoughts might fasten on. It had been chance
Always till now that had filled up the moment
With live specifics your hilarious comment
Discovered as it went along; and fed,
Laconic, quick, wherever it was led.
You improvised upon your own delight.
I think back to the scented summer night
We talked between our sleeping bags, below

A molten field of stars five years ago:
I was so tickled by your mind's light touch
I couldn't sleep, you made me laugh too much,
Though I was tired and begged you to leave off.

Now you were tired, and yet not tired enough
– Still hungry for the great world you were losing
Steadily in no season of your choosing –
And when at last the whole death was assured,
Drugs having failed, and when you had endured
Two weeks of an abominable constraint,
You faced it equably, without complaint,
Unwhimpering, but not at peace with it.
You'd lived as if your time was infinite:
You were not ready and not reconciled,
Feeling as uncompleted as a child
Till you had shown the world what you could do
In some ambitious role to be worked through,
A role your need for it had half-defined,
But never wholly, even in your mind.
You lacked the necessary ruthlessness,
The soaring meanness that pinpoints success.
We loved that lack of self-love, and your smile,
Rueful, at your own silliness.
                                        Meanwhile,
Your lungs collapsed, and the machine, unstrained,
Did all your breathing now. Nothing remained
But death by drowning on an inland sea
Of your own fluids, which it seemed could be
Kindly forestalled by drugs. Both could and would:
Nothing was said, everything understood,
At least by us. Your own concerns were not
Long-term, precisely, when they gave the shot

[467]

– You made local arrangements to the bed
And pulled a pillow round beside your head.
    And so you slept, and died, your skin gone grey,
Achieving your completeness, in a way.

Outdoors next day, I was dizzy from a sense
Of being ejected with some violence
From vigil in a white and distant spot
Where I was numb, into this garden plot
Too warm, too close, and not enough like pain.
I was delivered into time again
– The variations that I live among
Where your long body too used to belong
And where the still bush is minutely active.
You never thought your body was attractive,
Though others did, and yet you trusted it
And must have loved its fickleness a bit
Since it was yours and gave you what it could,
Till near the end it let you down for good,
Its blood hospitable to those guests who
Took over by betraying it into
The greatest of its inconsistencies
This difficult, tedious, painful enterprise.

Terminal

The eight years difference in age seems now
Disparity so wide between the two
That when I see the man who armoured stood
Resistant to all help however good
Now helped through day itself, eased into chairs,
Or else led step by step down the long stairs
With firm and gentle guidance by his friend,
Who loves him, through each effort to descend,
Each wavering, each attempt made to complete
An arc of movement and bring down the feet
As if with that spare strength he used to enjoy,
I think of Oedipus, old, led by a boy.

Still Life

I shall not soon forget
The greyish-yellow skin
To which the face had set:
Lids tight: nothing of his,
No tremor from within,
Played on the surfaces.

He still found breath, and yet
It was an obscure knack.
I shall not soon forget
The angle of his head,
Arrested and reared back
On the crisp field of bed,

Back from what he could neither
Accept, as one opposed,
Nor, as a life-long breather,
Consentingly let go,
The tube his mouth enclosed
In an astonished O.

The Reassurance

About ten days or so
After we saw you dead
You came back in a dream.
I'm all right now you said.

And it *was* you, although
You were fleshed out again:
You hugged us all round then,
And gave your welcoming beam.

How like you to be kind,
Seeking to reassure.
And, yes, how like my mind
To make itself secure.

Words for Some Ash

Poor parched man, we had to squeeze
Dental sponge against your teeth,
So that moisture by degrees
Dribbled to the mouth beneath.

Christmas Day your pupils crossed,
Staring at your nose's tip,
Seeking there the air you lost
Yet still gaped for, dry of lip.

Now you are a bag of ash
Scattered on a coastal ridge,
Where you watched the distant crash,
Ocean on a broken edge.

Death has wiped away each sense;
Fire took muscle, bone, and brains;
Next may rain leach discontents
From your dust, wash what remains

Deeper into damper ground
Till the granules work their way
Down to unseen streams, and bound
Briskly in the water's play;

May you lastly reach the shore,
Joining tide without intent,
Only worried any more
By the currents' argument.

Sacred Heart

For one who watches with too little rest
A body rousing fitfully to its pain
– The nerves like dull burns where the sheet has pressed –
Subsiding to dementia yet again;
For one who snatches what repose he can,
Exhausted by the fretful reflexes
Jerked from the torpor of a dying man,
Sleep is a fear, invaded as it is
By coil on coil of ominous narrative
In which specific isolated streaks,
Bright as tattoos, of inks that seem to live,
Shift through elusive patterns. Once in those weeks
You dreamt your dying friend hung crucified
In his front room, against the mantelpiece;
Yet it was Christmas, when you went outside
The shoppers bustled, bells rang without cease,
You smelt a sharp excitement on the air,
Crude itch of evergreen. But you returned
To find him still nailed up, mute sufferer
Lost in a trance of pain, toward whom you yearned.
When you woke up, you could not reconcile
The two conflicting scenes, indoors and out.
But it was Christmas. And parochial school
Accounted for the Dying God no doubt.

Now since his death you've lost the wish for sleep,
In which you might mislay the wound of feeling:
Drugged you drag grief from room to room and weep,
Preserving it from closure, from a healing
Into the novelty of glazed pink flesh.

We hear you stumble vision-ward above,
Keeping the edges open, bloody, fresh.

Wound, no – the heart, His Heart, broken with love.

An unfamiliar ticking makes you look
Down your left side where, suddenly apparent
Like a bright plate from an anatomy book
– In its snug housing, under the transparent
Planes of swept muscle and the barrelled bone –
The heart glows and you feel the holy heat:
The heart of hearts transplanted to your own
Losing rich purple drops with every beat.
Yet even as it does your vision alters,
The hallucination lighted through the skin
Begins to deaden (though still bleeding), falters,
And hardens to its evident origin
– A red heart from a cheap religious card,
Too smooth, too glossy, too securely cased!

Stopped in a crouch, you wearily regard
Each drop dilute into the waiting waste.

Her Pet

I walk the floor, read, watch a cop-show, drink,
Hear buses heave uphill through drizzling fog,
Then turn back to the pictured book to think
Of Valentine Balbiani and her dog:
She is reclining, reading, on her tomb;
But pounced, it tries to intercept her look,
Its front paws on her lap, as in this room
The cat attempts to nose beneath my book.

Her curls tight, breasts held by her bodice high,
Ruff crisp, mouth calm, hands long and delicate,
All in the pause of marble signify
A strength so lavish she can limit it.
She will not let her pet dog catch her eye
For dignity, and for a touch of wit.

Below, from the same tomb, is reproduced
A side-relief, in which she reappears
Without her dog, and everything is loosed –
Her hair down from the secret of her ears,
Her big ears, and her creased face genderless
Craning from sinewy throat. Death is so plain!
Her breasts are low knobs through the unbound dress.
In the worked features I can read the pain
She went through to get here, to shake it all,
Thinking at first that her full nimble strength
Hid like a little dog within recall,
Till to think so, she knew, was to pretend
And, hope dismissed, she sought out pain at length
And laboured with it to bring on its end.

Courtesies of the Interregnum

a memory of the Colonnades, Sept. 1986

He speaks of eating three hot meals a day
To bolster off the absence on its way.
In Juárez, too, a medicine is sold
That holds the immune cells firm, he has been told.
Expert of health, he watches every trend.
It truly must be difficult for my friend
To hold on to the substance that is him,
Once sternly regulated in the gym,
Prime flesh now softening on his giant frame.

When he gave weekly dinners here, we came
To this large white room with white furnishings,
Where in dim patience among handsome things
He awaits the day's event now – the late sun
At regular exercise, its daily run
Across the polished floorboards, tamed, discreet,
That swaggered over shoulders in the street.

Yet even while subdued to his pale room,
He rallies, smiles, I see he has become
The man I know – for suddenly aware
That he forgot his guest in his despair,
He is, confronted by a guest so fit,
Almost concerned lest I feel out of it,
Excluded from the invitation list
To the largest gathering of the decade, missed
From membership as if the club were full.
It is not that I am not eligible,
He gallantly implies. *He* is, for sure

– The athlete to be asked out one time more.
And he now, athlete-like, triumphs at length,
Though with not physical but social strength
Precisely exerted. He who might well cry
Reaches through such informal courtesy
To values grasped and shaped out as he goes,
Of which the last is bravery, for he knows
That even as he gets them in his grip
Context itself starts dizzyingly to slip.

To the Dead Owner of a Gym

I will remember well
The elegant decision
To that red line of tile
As margin round the showers
Of your gym, Norm,
In which so dashing a physique
As yours for several years
Gained muscle every week
With sharper definition.
Death on the other hand
Is rigid and,
Finally as it may define
An absence with its cutting line,
$$\text{Alas,}$$
$$\text{Lacks class.}$$

Memory Unsettled

Your pain still hangs in air,
Sharp motes of it suspended;
The voice of your despair –
That also is not ended:

When near your death a friend
Asked you what he could do,
'Remember me,' you said.
We will remember you.

Once when you went to see
Another with a fever
In a like hospital bed,
With terrible hothouse cough
And terrible hothouse shiver
That soaked him and then dried him,
And you perceived that he
Had to be comforted,

You climbed in there beside him
And hugged him plain in view,
Though you were sick enough,
And had your own fears too.

The J Car

Last year I used to ride the J CHURCH Line,
Climbing between small yards recessed with vine
– Their ordered privacy, their plots of flowers
Like blameless lives we might imagine ours.
Most trees were cut back, but some brushed the car
Before it swung round to the street once more
On which I rolled out almost to the end,
To 29th Street, calling for my friend.
    He'd be there at the door, smiling but gaunt,
To set out for the German restaurant.
There, since his sight was tattered now, I would
First read the menu out. He liked the food
In which a sourness and dark richness meet
For conflict without taste of a defeat,
As in the Sauerbraten. What he ate
I hoped would help him to put on some weight,
But though the crusted pancakes might attract
They did so more as concept than in fact,
And I'd eat his dessert before we both
Rose from the neat arrangement of the cloth,
Where the connection between life and food
Had briefly seemed so obvious if so crude.
Our conversation circumspectly cheerful,
We had sat here like children good but fearful
Who think if they behave everything might
Still against likelihood come out all right.
    But it would not, and we could not stay here:
Finishing up the Optimator beer
I walked him home through the suburban cool
By dimming shape of church and Catholic school,

Only a few, white, teenagers about.
After the four blocks he would be tired out.
I'd leave him to the feverish sleep ahead,
Myself to ride through darkened yards instead
Back to my health. Of course I simplify.
Of course. It tears me still that he should die
As only an apprentice to his trade,
The ultimate engagements not yet made.
His gifts had been withdrawing one by one
Even before their usefulness was done:
This optic nerve would never be relit;
The other flickered, soon to be with it.
Unready, disappointed, unachieved,
He knew he would not write the much-conceived
Much-hoped-for work now, nor yet help create
A love he might in full reciprocate.

To a Dead Graduate Student

The whole rich process of twined opposites,
Tendril round stalk, developing in tandem
Through tangled exquisite detail that knits
To a unique promise –
                          checked at random,
Killed, wasted. What a teacher you'd have made:
Your tough impatient mind, your flowering looks
Would have seduced the backward where they played,
Rebels like you, to share your love of books.

The Missing

Now as I watch the progress of the plague,
The friends surrounding me fall sick, grow thin,
And drop away. Bared, is my shape less vague
– Sharply exposed and with a sculpted skin?

I do not like the statue's chill contour,
Not nowadays. The warmth investing me
Led outward through mind, limb, feeling, and more
In an involved increasing family.

Contact of friend led to another friend,
Supple entwinement through the living mass
Which for all that I knew might have no end,
Image of an unlimited embrace.

I did not just feel ease, though comfortable:
Aggressive as in some ideal of sport,
With ceaseless movement thrilling through the whole,
Their push kept me as firm as their support.

But death – Their deaths have left me less defined:
It was their pulsing presence made me clear.
I borrowed from it, I was unconfined,
Who tonight balance unsupported here,

Eyes glaring from raw marble, in a pose
Languorously part-buried in the block,
Shins perfect and no calves, as if I froze
Between potential and a finished work.

– Abandoned incomplete, shape of a shape,
In which exact detail shows the more strange,
Trapped in unwholeness, I find no escape
Back to the play of constant give and change.

August 1987

Death's Door

Of course the dead outnumber us
— How their recruiting armies grow!
My mother archaic now as Minos,
She who died forty years ago.

After their processing, the dead
Sit down in groups and watch TV,
In which they must be interested,
For on it they see you and me.

These four, who though they never met
Died in one month, sit side by side
Together in front of the same set,
And all without a *TV Guide*.

Arms round each other's shoulders loosely,
Although they can feel nothing, who
When they unlearned their pain so sprucely
Let go of all sensation too.

Thus they watch friend and relative
And life here as they think it is
— In black and white, repetitive
As situation comedies.

With both delight and tears at first
They greet each programme on death's stations,
But in the end lose interest,
Their boredom turning to impatience.

'He misses me? He must be kidding
– This week he's sleeping with a cop.'
'All she reads now is *Little Gidding*.'
'They're getting old. I wish they'd stop.'

The habit of companionship
Lapses – they break themselves of touch:
Edging apart at arm and hip,
Till separated on the couch,

They woo amnesia, look away
As if they were not yet elsewhere,
And when snow blurs the picture they,
Turned, give it a belonging stare.

Snow blows out toward them, till their seat
Filling with flakes becomes instead
Snow-bank, snow-landscape, and in that
They find themselves with all the dead,

Where passive light from snow-crust shows them
Both Minos circling and my mother.
Yet none of the recruits now knows them,
Nor do they recognize each other,

They have been so superbly trained
Into the perfect discipline
Of an archaic host, and weaned
From memory briefly barracked in.

A Blank

The year of griefs being through, they had to merge
In one last grief, with one last property:
To view itself like loosened cloud lose edge,
And pull apart, and leave a voided sky.

Watching Victorian porches through the glass,
From the 6 bus, I caught sight of a friend
Stopped on a corner-kerb to let us pass,
A four-year-old blond child tugging his hand,
Which tug he held against with a slight smile.
I knew the smile from certain passages
Two years ago, thus did not know him well,
Since they took place in my bedroom and his.

A sturdy-looking admirable young man.
He said 'I chose to do this with my life.'
Casually met he said it of the plan
He undertook without a friend or wife.

Now visibly tugged upon by his decision,
Wayward and eager. So this was his son!
What I admired about his self-permission
Was that he turned from nothing he had done,
Or was, or had been, even while he transposed
The expectations he took out at dark
— Of Eros playing, features undisclosed —
Into another pitch, where he might work

With the same melody, and opted so
To educate, permit, guide, feed, keep warm,
And love a child to be adopted, though
The child was still a blank then on a form.

The blank was flesh now, running on its nerve,
This fair-topped organism dense with charm,
Its braided muscle grabbing what would serve,
His countering pull, his own devoted arm.

Postscript and Notes

In putting this collection together, I have omitted a dozen poems I find stupid or badly written, and I have added a dozen which didn't make it into the books but now seem to me worth printing. Grateful acknowledgements are therefore made to the editors and publishers of the following periodicals and pamphlets: *Critical Quarterly*, *Gay Times*, *Massachusetts Review*, *Numbers*, *Observer*, *San Francisco Sentinel*, *Times Literary Supplement*, ZYZZYVA; *At the Barriers* (NADJA), *The Hurtless Trees* (Jordan Davies), *The Missed Beat* (Gruffyground Press and Janus Press), *Undesirables* (Pig Press). Three of the poems from *Fighting Terms* are revisions; the other poems from it appear as in the first edition.

A few notes might help:

'Lofty in the Palais de Danse': the unfortunate youth is constantly being transferred (posted) from one army camp to another.

'A Mirror for Poets': the Paphlagonian king is a character in Sidney's *Arcadia*.

'On the Move': most English people nowadays give 'toward' two syllables, whereas Americans, like the Elizabethans, treat it as one. In my early books I was still an English poet, not yet Anglo-American.

'In Santa Maria del Popolo': I am not sure where I read this account of Caravaggio's death. I later found that it is not the accepted one.

'The Annihilation of Nothing': the image in line 20 refers to what happened in an oil lamp when the lighted wick was turned up too high.

'Innocence': I should point out that dedicating a poem to someone does not necessarily mean it is about him.

'The Byrnies': a byrnie was a chainmail shirt; a nicker was a water monster.

'L'Epreuve' was about taking mescaline. Paul Bowles had pointed out the two senses of the word *épreuve*.

'Misanthropos': I found Anton Schmidt in Hannah Arendt's *Eichmann in Jerusalem*.

'The Vigil of Corpus Christi' took its start from a sequence in Eisenstein's mutilated footage shown as *Qué Viva Mexico*.

'Back to Life': an English keeper is an American groundskeeper; and a lime-tree in England is a linden in America.

'The Inside-Outside Game' was based on an idea by Donald Moyer.

'For Signs': by a chicken bowl I simply meant a bowl from which chickens on a farm eat or drink.

'The Sand Man' had been a union-organizer in San Francisco, I was told, until he suffered a brain injury as result of a beating.

The speaker of 'Faustus Triumphant' has an amphetamine problem.

'Jack Straw's Castle': the Oxford dictionary defines Jack Straw as 'a "straw man"; a man of no substance, worth, or consideration.' A pub in Hampstead is called Jack Straw's Castle, but I just took the name and intended no allusions to Hampstead in the poem. Little Ease was a cell in which you could not stand, sit, or lie.

'Yoko' was a Newfoundland dog. The poem takes place on July 4, in New York, hence the fireworks.

'Bally *Power Play*': pinball machines are vanishing so fast it is necessary to point out that this is the name of a specific model.

In 'The Menace', the quotation from Gregory Bateson comes from his *Steps to an Ecology of Mind*.

'The Victim': her name was Nancy Spingarn.

'A Drive to Los Alamos': the novelist was William Burroughs.

'Night Taxi': the driver must be glad, at the end of the poem, that rain will bring him more business.

'Punch Rubicundus': my school was one of many with a periodicals room containing bound volumes of the comic magazine *Punch* going back for many a year. The third section of the poem refers to a detail on Richard Doyle's original cover-design, which it still had in my childhood. Uncle Willie was Pound's name for Yeats.

'At the Barriers': the street fair this commemorates took place in August, 1988, in San Francisco. At least two of Ben Jonson's masques were composed in connection with 'barriers' (which for him meant an exhibition of tilting). I use barriers in a modern sense but retain the associations of a masque.

'The Differences': the poet is Guido Cavalcanti.

Some of the poems in the fourth part of *The Man with Night Sweats* refer to friends who died before their time. For the record – for *my* record if for no one else's, because they were not famous people – I wish to name them here: 'The Reassurance' and 'Lament' are about Allan Noseworthy; 'Terminal' and 'Words for Some Ash', Jim Lay; 'Still Life', Larry Hoyt; 'To the Dead Owner of a Gym' and 'Courtesies of the Interregnum', Norm Rathweg; 'Memory Unsettled', 'To a Dead Graduate Student' and 'The J Car', Charlie Hinkle, lines from whose *Poems* are quoted as an epigraph. Two more, Lonnie Leard and Allen Day, enter less directly into other poems.

'Her Pet': the tomb is by Germain Pilon. It is illustrated in Michael Levey's *High Renaissance* (Penguin Books), p. 129.

Index of Titles